Department of the Environment

The Impact of Environmental Improvements on Urban Regeneration

PIEDA plc
Planning Economic and Development Consultants

London: HMSO

ISBN 0 11 753110 3

Contents

Preface

This report was commissioned by the Department of the Environment from Pieda plc, planning economic and development consultants. The project was managed by David Edwards and the team included Philip Challen and Christine Lalley.

Steven Batey was the nominated officer for the Department of the Environment and we are grateful to him, to members of the steering group for their advice and support; also to DOE Regional Offices, Local Authorities, Development Corporations, companies and others who kindly assisted us in this study. The views expressed in the report remain those of the consultants.

Executive Summary

Report

This is the final report of a study commissioned by the Department of the Environment to assess the impact of Environmental Improvement Projects (EIPs) on urban regeneration. The report examines the extent to which EIPs achieve economic regeneration objectives by influencing potential investors in inner urban areas, the capacity for EIPs to assist regeneration, and the policy implications.

The overall conclusion is that EIPs can make a practical contribution to urban renewal in attracting and supporting private investment. The impact of EIPs is, however, substantially influenced by economic and market circumstances, together with the physical constraints on development and investment for an individual area or site and whether these are addressed by the improvements.

Environmental improvement projects

EIPs with economic objectives are projects whose main objectives are the physical improvement of the urban fabric for the purposes of attraction of private sector investment rather than the simple consideration of visual amenity. This includes environmental works such as ground treatment, site access and services, as well as more general amenity improvements. The projects examined were drawn from the Urban Programme, Derelict Land Grant and Urban Development Corporation regimes. However, the intention was to examine the general lessons from environmental improvements rather than compare the different policy regimes.

EIPs influence on the development process

The study shows that EIPs have the potential to influence the development process and investment decisions. This is shown in both interviews with developers and the range of successful case studies examined.

EIPs exert the strongest influence on development investment when addressing the following development factors:

- **Site and Premises Availability**: EIPs assist through land assembly, acquisition, clearance and sale to developers

- **Access, Transport and Infrastructure**: EIPs can provide road access, pedestrianisation and infrastructure to support development

- **Land and Development Costs**: EIPs can provide a subsidy to underwrite development viability

- **Planning and Economic Policies**: EIPs can provide mutual reinforcement to planning and economic development policies for urban regeneration.

EIPs exert a weaker influence on development investment when addressing the following factors:

- **Location and accommodation requirements:** these are functions of external economic and property market demand factors and not amenable to influence by EIPs, except indirectly in the longer term as cumulative investment in an area reinforces demand.

- **Environmental requirements:** changes in a location's visual environment or amenity were not found sufficient alone to induce investment, but may reinforce investment decisions, particularly if linked to development. Similar considerations apply to improvements to buildings and landscaping.

- **Availability of finance:** the majority of EIPs are initiated and undertaken by the public sector which restricts the participation and attraction of the private sector

- **Risk and timing:** improving an area through EIPs can reinforce investment decisions. Overall developers' perceptions of the risk and timing on decisions were that EIPs were supportive, but not critical.

- **Capital and rental values:** EIPs have little impact on values in weak property markets, but can assist in encouraging increased occupancy of accommodation.

However, the influence of EIPs on development also reflects different types of developer activity:

- **Niche developers:** specialist inner area developers tend to work within the constraints of the existing urban environment with EIPs exercising less influence.

- **Urban renewal developers:** with an emphasis on comprehensive physical urban renewal to create a new environment, EIPs can support projects with site assembly, clearance and highways and services.

- **General developers:** EIPs support investment through site works and services, but also help reinforce investment decisions through improvements to inner areas' general amenity.

There are common themes which are evident in the impact of EIPs on development investment:

- External economic and property market forces influence development demand and therefore the overall potential impact of EIPs. EIPs are most effective when there is underlying property demand such that the local economy can support new development.

- EIPs have their greatest impact where they are applied as a direct support to development investment, removing physical development constraints, such as providing access, services and infrastructure, removing contamination and making sites available.

- EIPs have a weaker impact where applied to visual improvements, particularly without direct relationship to physical development where influences are too diffuse and subtle except to act as reinforcement for investment decisions.

The impact of EIPs on urban regeneration

Overall, the case studies examined in this study were successful in their objectives of attracting investment to inner urban areas, showing that EIPs have the capacity to support economic regeneration. However, success requires the translation of the general lessons about the circumstances in which they have potential, identified above, into practical action. Two sets of factors are important here:

- characteristics: area or site led approach, use and policy regime

- project features: context and application.

(i) Characteristics

Selection of the appropriate EIP structure needs to have reference to the characteristics and requirements of individual locations.

Area and project led approach: the appropriate choice requires a clear assessment of whether development potential and constraints are best addressed at area or site level.

Uses: different uses have affected the capacity of EIPs to influence investment decisions. Retailing and higher value commercial uses are more sensitive to their environs and respond to more general area wide programmes. Residential, leisure and industrial uses are more focused on immediate environs and the individual site considerations.

Policy Regimes:

Urban Programme the regime's strengths have been area-based and public sector project-based schemes. Success has been dependent on rigorous assessment followed by a clear development plan, including clear objectives, programming and planning, rather than incremental programme evolution.

Derelict Land Grant has been a major source of site specific land reclamation by the public sector for subsequent private sector development. The impact of area based projects with an amenity emphasis might have been increased if linked to private sector participation and support. Linkages with development have tended to be weak for amenity projects.

Urban Development Corporations integration of EIPs with planning and economic policies, together with strong promotion and an emphasis on site provision, access, amenity works and infrastructure has worked very successfully overall. Projects which have had a general amenity rather than development focus have tended to have a lesser impact.

(ii) Features

The application of EIPs were most effective when the following features were addressed:

- **Area and project assessment:** a rigorous assessment of economic and development potential at project inception provides clear definition of objectives and constraints and a framework of EIP specification and implementation.

- **Promotion and consultation:** the strongest projects have involved continuing consultation and promotion throughout their programme.

- **Development:** projects which have included site provision and development have had a very strong impact in providing a focus for investment and demonstrating a commitment to the location.

- **Highways and infrastructure:** these have enhanced the accessibility of locations, removed constraints and provided a framework for development and amenity improvements.

- **Property rehabilitation:** concentration of grant assistance on key frontages and on the basis of sustainable economic development has been successful in attracting investment from owners and occupiers.

- **Amenity improvements**: these have had the strongest impact reinforcing other projects, in particular development and improvement to site access, and targeted at attracting investment from general developers and investors after highway and site improvement works have been completed.

- **Policy linkage:** complementing planning and economic policies have reinforced EIPs and diversified funding sources.

- **Partnership:** recently there have been a limited number of formal partnerships between public and private sectors to provide a link between public sector EIP initiatives and private sector investment.

- **Grant assistance:** EIPs have been important in providing subsidy to development through on-site works as reclamation.

- **Programming and timescale:** where these are determined at the outset, EIPs have a clear focus and objective. Without these, extended area based programmes can lose direction.

- **Funding mixture:** the application of a range of complementary policy and funding regimes allows an extended funding base and increased resources.

Implications for inner city policies and programmes

EIPs with economic objectives have been successful in supporting urban regeneration. The key implications for programmes and policies are summarised below:

- **Area and project assessment:** before initiating EIPs an area assessment is required to establish the location's economic and development potential, the constraints and appropriate scale of EIP response. The linkage between economic EIPs' objectives and potential investment needs to be clearly defined.

- **Use:** emphasis should be placed on the appropriate EIP structure where development uses are predisposed to such support - for example usage of area based approaches for retail and higher value commercial uses, and more site specific approaches for residential and industrial uses.

- **Programming and timetable:** area based or multi-project EIPs require a programme for implementation to ensure coherent planning, co-ordination and effective promotion over their timetable.

- **Consultation and promotion:** there is a requirement for effective promotion and consultation with the private sector at each stage of the EIP programme extending from formal partnerships for longer projects, through to newsletters and promotion of grant assistance, and preparation of development briefs to provide full information on potential opportunities.

- **Highways, infrastructure and services:** adequate highways and services are essential to support economic development. This requires co-ordination of EIP or complementary action through the programmes to provide an effective services framework as a priority for investment.

- **Site availability and development:** following highways, site availability is a pre-requisite for attracting development investment, and needs to be integrated within an area development framework.

- **Amenity improvements:** these need to be linked with highways, development and site promotion to attract general developer investment. Without a clear focus on specific development and investment projects, the economic impact of amenity improvements is dissipated and less effective.

- **Planning and economic framework:** EIPs should be supported by complementary planning and economic policies to provide a comprehensive policy approach and supporting the promotion and development of the area.

- **Fund mixing:** EIP specification needs to identify the potential for attracting complementary funding with the aim of diversifying and extending the funding base.

In summary, the impact of EIPs with economic objectives depends on a clear assessment of economic and development potential and the constraints to be addressed, with an emphasis on infrastructure, site availability and clearance and amenity improvements which are linked to development.

1 The report

1.1 This is the final report of the study commissioned by the Department of the Environment to assess the impact of environmental improvements on urban regeneration.

The study

1.2 The objectives of the study are:

- to assess whether Environmental Improvement Projects, promoted for economic regeneration reasons, achieve their objectives

- to assess the extent to which environmental improvements affect the attitudes and perceptions of potential investors towards an area

- to assess the capacity of environmental improvements to help regenerate inner city areas, and the scale and capacity of environmental projects required

- the policy implications in terms of cost-effectiveness and targeting.

1.3 The study is designed to seek best practice in Environmental Improvement Projects and the lessons which may be applied to future projects.

1.4 The focus for this study is the impact of environmental improvements on urban regeneration as measured by development investment in areas which have benefited from such public expenditure.

1.5 Three urban policy programmes were included in the study:

- Urban Programme (UP)

- Derelict Land Grant (DLG)

- Urban Development Corporations (UDC's).

1.6 The Urban Development Grant and City Grant regimes were the subject of a separate study and were not reviewed here, except in the context of their interaction with Environmental Improvement Projects.

1.7 In each case, the intention was to examine the general lessons from environmental improvements rather than compare the different policy regimes.

1.8 The findings of the study are designed to inform the management of Inner City programmes and provide an input to wider policy considerations.

Environmental improvement projects

1.9 Environmental Improvement Projects are a very general grouping. There is no consistent formal definition of EIPs across the range of urban policy programmes examined here. For the purposes of this study we examine projects whose main objectives are:

- the physical improvement of land and buildings; and

- the attraction of private sector investment.

1.10 The study therefore presents a broader examination than a definition purely restricted to considerations of visual amenity. The definition includes the full range of environmental works including elements such as ground treatment, site services and access improvements.

1.11 This approach:

- is consistent with the broad interpretation of the definition of environmental projects in urban policy; and

- implicit in environmental projects with the objective of attracting development investment where usually visual amenity alone is not the principal feature.

1.12 The separation of environmental projects with urban renewal economic objectives, and economic projects with environmental objectives is in practice a fine line, often dependent on the subjective weighting of relative objectives and reflecting different policy programme administration, local programme priorities and the individual project context. This has required the consultants to take judgements on the inclusion of individual case studies. However, the focus of the study has remained the examination of Environmental Improvement Projects and their assessment in terms of economic regeneration objectives.

Policy context

1.13 EIPs with economic objectives are drawn from a range of different budgets within the policy programmes examined. The different origins of EIPs are illustrated in Figure 1.1 and outlined opposite.

Urban Programme

1.14 Urban Programme projects are divided under three headings.

- Environmental

- Economic

- Social.

1.15 Projects are assigned to each group according to their principal objective, although projects will often have associated or subsidiary objectives which are relevant to the other groups. Attribution of some projects between Environmental and Economic headings is a fine judgement based on the relative weighting of objectives. This is particularly so in the case of physical development projects where environmental and economic development are often linked.

Figure 1.1 Environmental improvement projects programme context

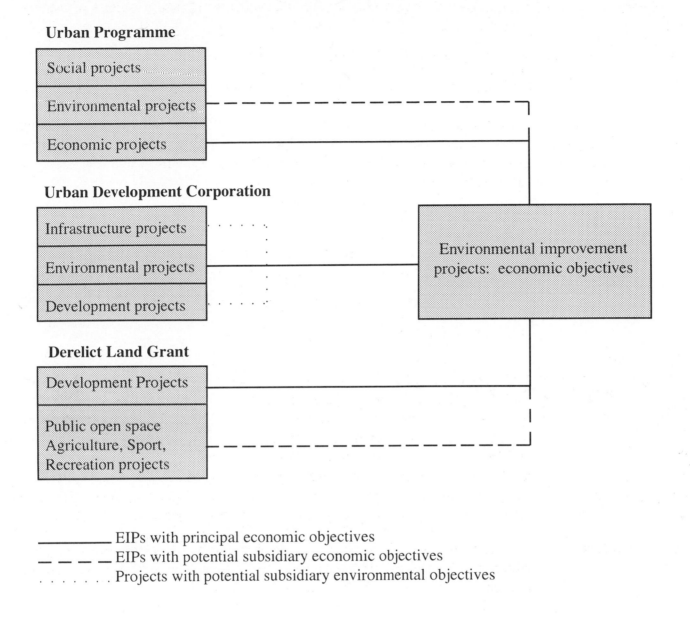

_____ EIPs with principal economic objectives
_ _ _ _ EIPs with potential subsidiary economic objectives
. . . . Projects with potential subsidiary environmental objectives

1.16 We have examined projects from both Environmental and Economic categories, but with an emphasis on the latter. This reflects the position that EIPs, promoted for economic regeneration reasons, tend to be identified as Economic rather than Environmental projects, with Environmental projects essentially promoted for reasons of amenity.

1.17 Under the Urban Programme in 1991-92 a total of £271 million was allocated through Inner Area Programmes (IAP) by the 57 Programme Authorities on approved projects. £126 million (46%) was spent on economic projects, and £52 million (19%) on environmental projects. The balance (35%) was applied to social and housing objectives. 75% of the cost of capital Urban Programme projects is funded by grant, the remaining 25% by Supplementary Credit Approvals, allowing Local Authorities to borrow.

1.18 The range of environmental projects include the following:

Development: acquisition, conversion or refurbishment of properties by the Local Authority

Building improvements: grants (and loans) to owners and occupiers for external repair or improvement of properties

Roads and pavements: repairs and improvement of roads and highways

Landscaping: hard and soft landscaping for inner area projects including planting, street furniture, and top-up funding for site improvements.

1.19 Expenditure under the Urban Programme budgets for the individual Local Authorities can be distinguished between project specific allocations and block allocations. The latter are consolidated funds which are applied to small scale (up to £10,000 for the private sector) generic projects, for example, face lift grants for building improvements, and may be applied at the Local Authorities' discretion in accordance with criteria agreed by the Department.

Urban Development Corporations

1.20 Urban Development Corporations annual programmes differentiate between environmental and other categories of expenditure. As in the case with Urban Programme, however, Environmental Improvement Projects are spread across a range of budgetary classes, depending on the objectives of individual projects and their classification.

1.21 Urban Development Corporation budgets are divided into three groups:

- Development

- Infrastructure

- Environment.

1.22 As in the case of Urban Programme, projects often have multiple objectives. Development and Infrastructure groups are inextricably linked to direct economic objectives. Environmental projects often have less direct economic or development outputs, but this very much depends on individual projects. Major projects will often draw on expenditure from more than one group budget.

1.23 We have examined projects which are drawn from the Environmental Group budget which have the explicit objective of attracting development investment.

1.24 Urban Development Corporations are designed to achieve regeneration by bringing buildings and land back to effective use. The total expenditure for the 10 Urban Development Corporations was some £338 million (1988-89) before receipts, with additional assistance to the private sector through City Grant and Inner Urban Areas grants.

Development Land Grant

1.25 This regime is in contrast with the other two described, having no economic or environmental classification. The formal definition of derelict land is:

> 'land so damaged by industrial or other development that is incapable of beneficial use without treatment'.

This implies that grant assisted projects are all to an extent environmental as a consequence of treatment of damaged land.

1.26 The regime distinguishes projects between:

- hard end use: where reclaimed land is redeveloped as housing, commercial or other forms of built development

- soft end use: where reclaimed land is left undeveloped, for example, for agriculture, or public open space or leisure.

1.27 In practical terms 'hard end use' might be considered as essentially economic, but 'soft end uses' may also impact on development perceptions of an area, and therefore have indirect economic outputs.

1.28 Derelict Land Grant finances approved schemes for derelict land reclamation to return it to effective use.

> **Public sector:** 100% grant assistance to Local Authorities for land acquisition and reclamation with after value proceeds off set against the grant.

> **Private sector:** 80% grant assistance for reclamation works net of any increase in after value of the site.

1.29 Lower levels of assistance apply for approved schemes outside Assisted Areas and Derelict Land Clearance Areas.

1.30 The total annual resources for DLG are some £77 million (1989-90), of which £66 million (86%) was paid to the public sector, and the balance of £11 million (14%) to private sector schemes. 1,487 hectares in total was reclaimed: 61% for hard end use development (commercial, residential, and mixed use), and the balance for soft end use (39%) (public open space, sport and leisure, agriculture).

Study methodology

1.31 The study methodology to assess whether Environmental Improvement Projects with economic regeneration objectives were successful in attracting development investment sought to identify the potential influences of EIPs on the development process, and then test these potential influences in practice through a survey of developers and case studies.

Development process

1.32 This examines the potential of EIPs to influence development factors and sets out a framework of potential impacts from assessment. This is discussed in Section 2.

Developer survey

1.33 This takes the assessment framework for potential impacts and tests these through a structured interview programme with selected developers who have invested in urban regeneration projects. The aim was to identify the influence and importance of EIPs on development decisions and whether this was in turn influenced according to individual developers, locations or types of development. The findings of the survey are examined in Section 3.

Case studies

1.34 A selection of EIP case studies were assessed to test the potential impact of EIPs on development decisions in practice, and to identify the lessons of success and best practice. The case studies were drawn from six regions with two regions assigned to each of the policy programmes. They were selected to demonstrate the success of EIPs and were chosen in consultation with the public agencies involved. The assessment involved interviews with DoE Regional Offices, Local Authorities, investors, developers, occupiers and agents. The assessment framework and approach are given in Section 4. Area wide projects are summarised in Section 5. Site specific projects are summarised in Section 6.

Impact of environmental improvements

1.35 This takes the assessment framework of potential EIP impact on development activity and compares this with the findings of the developer survey and case studies to identify the practical influences of EIPs, and how these may change depending on the nature of the project and its context. The findings are set out in Section 7.

Conclusions

1.36 This sets out the study conclusions on whether EIP activity promotes development investment and relevant conditions. On this basis the recommendations for policy are made. The conclusions and recommendations are given in Section 8.

2 Environmental improvements and the development process

2.1   This section reviews the principal factors in the development process and their relationship with Environmental Improvement Projects (EIPs). This is to identify the key factors which may be susceptible to influence through EIPs, and as a consequence promote the attraction of development investment. These factors provide the framework for testing developers' perceptions of EIPs, and assessing the impact of EIPs in the case studies reviewed.

Development process

2.2   If EIPs are to influence the investment then it is necessary to understand how the elements of the development process might be influenced.

2.3   Development is an output of property market supply and demand factors. A simplified model of the process is shown in Figure 2.1.

2.4   The process can be divided into four elements:

- **Demand Factors:** these relate to the property requirements of occupiers, investors and developers and reflect the wider economic structure of the area, choice of property and individual's operational needs.

- **Supply Factors:** these relate to the supply of sites and premises, their attributes, and their location and accessibility.

- **Perceptions:** the information on supply and demand factors available to decision-takers is limited and incomplete. Property decisions also involve subjective judgements. Perceptions are important in influencing how supply and demand information is interpreted and investment decisions are taken.

- **Development viability:** based on interpretation of the earlier elements, investors can make assessments as to potential returns against costs, and a judgement can be made as to viability.

2.5   These elements are examined below with reference to the potential influence of EIPs. It will be seen that the potential impact of EIPs is focused on removing constraints on supply factors and financial assistance to allow locations to compete for private sector investment.

Figure 2.1 Property development model

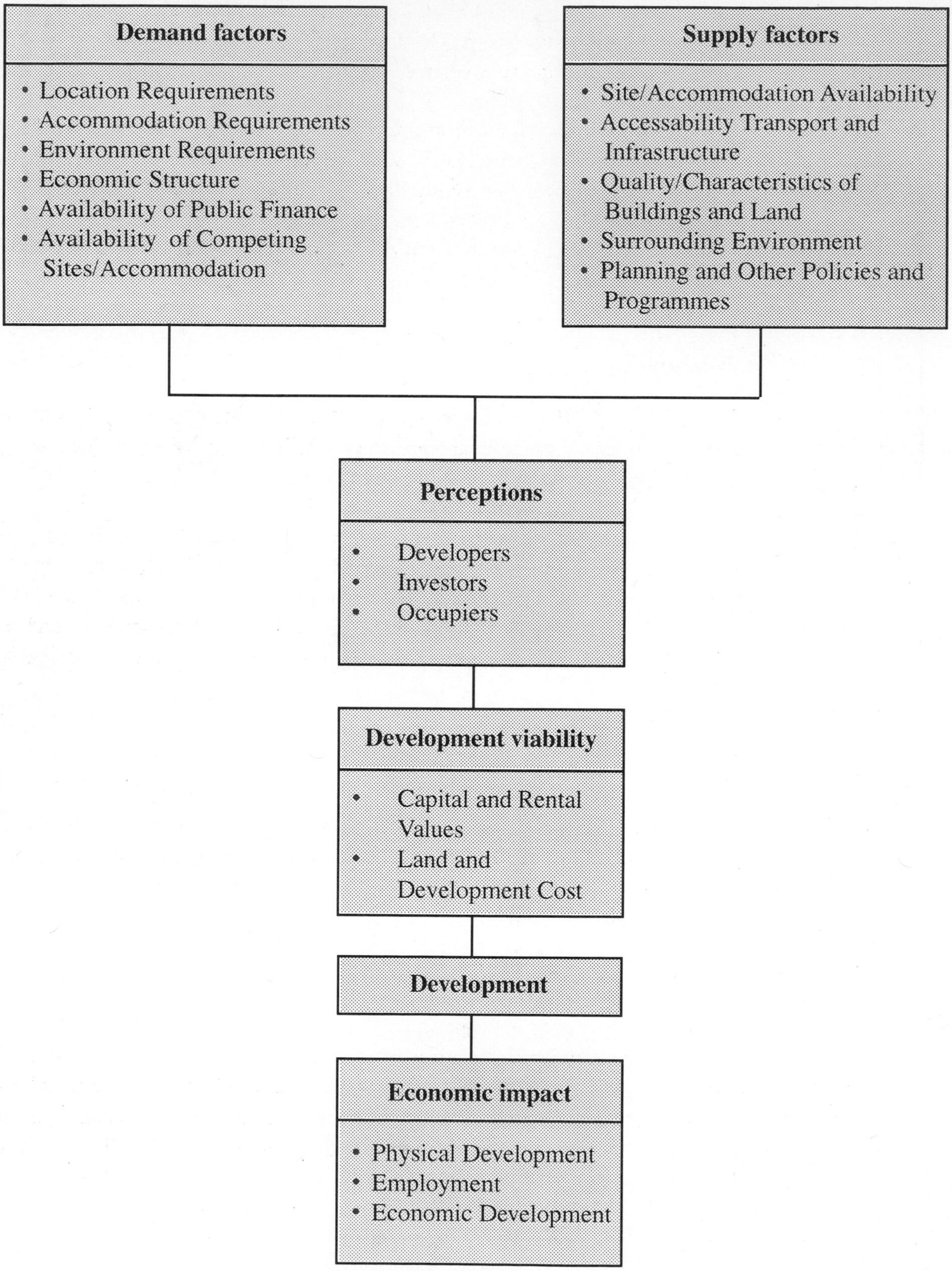

Demand factors

- Location Requirements
- Accommodation Requirements
- Environment Requirements
- Economic Structure
- Availability of Public Finance
- Availability of Competing Sites/Accommodation

Supply factors

- Site/Accommodation Availability
- Accessability Transport and Infrastructure
- Quality/Characteristics of Buildings and Land
- Surrounding Environment
- Planning and Other Policies and Programmes

Perceptions

- Developers
- Investors
- Occupiers

Development viability

- Capital and Rental Values
- Land and Development Cost

Development

Economic impact

- Physical Development
- Employment
- Economic Development

Demand factors

Location and accommodation requirements

2.6   EIPs are unlikely to change the basic locational and accommodation requirements of occupiers.   No matter how attractive a particular environment may be created, if it cannot meet location and accommodation requirements it is unlikely to attract investment.   In this context location is often cited as the prime consideration in property investment decisions.

2.7   Many urban regeneration areas are in inner city locations which are by definition relatively accessible.   However, even short distances can be a significant deterrent.   Location and accommodation requirements are not absolutes, but will be weighted against an area's other attributes and of other locations.   In seeking to revive investment in an area the principles of location and accessability are important.

Environmental requirements

2.8   Alongside the basic demand factors of location and accommodation environmental requirements are less easily defined.   Attributes may include visual amenity, public safety, taste and fashion.

2.9   Changes in taste and demand are evidenced, for example, in the growth of residential development in inner city locations associated with waterfront or docklands projects, and the return in England and Wales of demand for City Centre living.   Such change reflects a range of economic, demographic and cultural influences which EIPs at the general level may have reinforced, but are but one factor.

Economic structure

2.10   If EIPs are successful in their economic objectives, this will feed back into an area's prosperity and influence its economic structure and demand conditions. This influence can only be achieved indirectly, and is only one of a range of factors which will induce change over time.

Availability of public finance

2.11   There are limited cases where public sector financial assistance will, of itself, attract development demand. Enterprise Zones, which attract specialist tax driven investors, are a key example. For EIPs, the range of forms assistance, the project specific rather than general availability of assistance, and the limited access for the private sector to direct EIP assistance have not encouraged this.

Supply factors

Site and premises availability

2.12 The availability of land and property is a prerequisite if development investment is to be attracted. Public agencies frequently acquire ownership and interests in land to enable EIPs to be undertaken, for disposal to developers thereafter. The creation and marketing of development opportunities can attract private sector investment which would otherwise overlook projects because of uncertainty, timescale, cost and lack of information.

Site access, transport and infrastructure

2.13 Provision or improvement of access, for example pedestrianisation, is a feature of some EIPs. Such improvements may both enhance the external environment and provide a cost subsidy to development works.

2.14 On a broader scale provision of services and improvements to the road network are often an integral element of site reclamation and environmental improvement.

Quality and characteristics of buildings and land

2.15 The quality and characteristics of buildings and land are a consideration in the development process. These may include architectural or other features which provide the property with inherent qualities. EIPs can be applied to assist in safeguarding or restoring buildings' external features through repair or cleaning, or enhancing a site through landscaping. The wider effects can be to provide a subsidy to building works and enhancement of the environs.

Surrounding environment

2.16 The quality and characteristics of the surrounding environment are also a factor in influencing development investment. An attractive environment can be promoted to potential occupiers and users, and provides evidence of a stable local economy as a basis for long term investment. As with other environmental factors, the emphasis placed on this by developers, investors and occupiers varies and is often very subjective.

Planning policies

2.17 Planning policies influence the supply and availability of sites and property for development: by restriction, through Development Control, and through promotion with other programmes, identifying development opportunities and the co-ordination of supporting action. It is in the case of the latter that EIPs may be integrated in support of wider planning and economic development programmes co-ordinated to attract investment.

2.18 Perceptions inform the trade-off of demand requirements and supply attributes. EIPs may influence change in certain demand and supply factors, but in addition encourage change in development and investment perceptions.

Perceptions

Risk and timing

2.19 The influence of an enhanced environment may mitigate perceptions of investment risk. The programming of environmental works, or their initiation may encourage perceptions that the area is 'improving'. Developers may be encouraged to anticipate potential impacts of EIPs and commit investment to an area, or to bring forward the timing of development.

Profile

2.20 EIPs, and their association with particular buildings or public sector agencies, may influence developers' perceptions. Developers on large scale projects may perceive corporate benefits of association with the schemes which induce their initial involvement, even when the prospects of a commercial return were not certain. For example with some 'flagship' Urban Development Corporation schemes there is prestige in association with urban renewal agencies with a significant corporate presence.

Development viability

Capital and rental values

2.21 Capital and rental values may respond to EIPs. This may be a direct consequence of the enhanced amenity or environment achieved in a particular development. It may be a more indirect consequence of change in perceptions of a particular area, as noted earlier, or more locally with improvement of adjoining sites and buildings. Importantly in relatively depressed property markets the impact may not necessarily show in enhanced rental or capital values, but through the attraction of development investment, increased levels of sales or lettings, and a consequent decline in vacancy. In particular, it is often very difficult to demonstrate uplifts in values where evidence of the property market was previously very limited, and to attribute change to EIPs independent of other factors.

Land and development costs

2.22 EIPs linked to individual developments often provide a direct development subsidy to achieve commercial viability or to allow an improved development specification. In this context it is also important to have reference to other subsidy or grant mechanisms, for example City Grant, or ERDF assistance and their inter-relationship and effectiveness.

Development investment and EIPs: a framework for assessment

2.23 The potential range of EIP impacts on the factors which underlie development investment is substantial. It extends from the most immediate and easily measured, cost, through to more subtle impacts such as perceptions of risk and development profile. Further, these impacts may be manifest in different combinations. In these circumstances, evidence or perceptions of impact may be significantly understated, or may only become evident when initial works are substantially discounted.

2.24 We have taken the development factors discussed above and where there is potential for direct impact through EIPs identified, shown this in a framework for assessment. This is summarised in Figure 2.2. The impact of EIPs on these factors and their importance is examined subsequently in practice through a survey of developers and case studies.

Figure 2.2 EIP Framework: Potential Impact

Factor		Potential EIP Impact	Features
Demand Factors	Locational requirements		No potential for impact
	Accommodation requirements		No potential for impact
	Environmental requirements	○	General influence on trends and tastes
	Economic structure	○	Indirect influence through attraction of new investment
	Availability of public finance	○	Indirect influence as limited grants directly available to the private sector development
Supply Factors	Site and premises availability	●	Creation and marketing of development opportunities
	Site access, transport and infrastructure	●	Enhanced external environment, and possible cost subsidy
	Quality and characteristics of buildings and land	●	Reclamation of sites and rehabilitation of buildings
	Surrounding environment	●	Enhancement of area environment
	Planning and economic policies	●	Reinforcement of planning and economic policies and programmes
Perceptions	Risks and timing	●	Encouragement of investment in an area; perceptions of area improving
	Profile	●	Corporate benefits of association with public agencies and urban renewal
Development viability	Capital and rental values	●	Uplifts in values through environmental improvements
	Land and development costs	●	Development subsidy through EIP assistance

Note: Indirect Impact ○   direct Impact ●

12

3 Development perceptions of environmental improvements

3.1   Developers undertake a pivotal role in urban regeneration acting with occupiers and investors. Correct judgements result in schemes successfully occupied and the investments created either sold or retained.

3.2   An interview programme of developers who have had involvement with urban regeneration developments was undertaken. The purpose of the survey was to investigate:

- the relative importance of the individual development factors which were identified earlier as having the potential to be influenced by EIPs

- whether EIPs were perceived by developers as having an impact on development factors and influencing their development investment decisions.

The developers who participated in the interview programme are listed in Appendix I.

3.3   Developers have different backgrounds and adopt different approaches and specialisms which reflect individual strengths and interests. Three broad categories of inner area developer can be identified, although these are not exclusive and tend to extend into each other:

- Niche

- Urban renewal

- General

These are discussed below and the general relationship to EIPs reviewed.

3.4   We selected developers from each category to see whether perceptions of EIPs differed according to the type of developer, and therefore whether this should inform the application of EIPs in terms of the type of project and developer who might be attracted.

Niche developers

3.5   Niche developers include a limited number of specialist national developers or their subsidiaries. Developers in this category, and often local developers with similar characteristics, focus their experience and expertise on exploiting existing inner area urban renewal markets. There is a close understanding of local market conditions, and the ability to tailor development according to existing underlying demand.

3.6   This may include specialist forms of development: managed workspace, mixed commercial/residential uses, partnership housing and other forms of residential development such as shared-equity or rent-purchase projects. However, there is a constraint on such projects where release of developer's equity through sale to occupiers or investors (for re-investment in other schemes) is not readily achievable. Residential schemes with direct sales to occupiers do not present such problems.

3.7   Developers in this category tend to work within the existing urban framework rather than seeking to modify the external environment. Emphasis is put on using other factors to advantage.

- Location remains important, with developments often on the edge of the central area, with good access to City Centre services and transport links.

- Buildings which have an intrinsic quality or character are preferred. They project the profile of the development without reference necessarily to the surrounding environment.

- Low site values and ease of site acquisition are pre-requisites to offset development risk and cost.

3.8   Niche developers are often one of the first investors in inner city areas, as their projects are typically free standing and independent of supporting environmental or infrastructure works. Their success will attract other developers to the area and has the potential to generate a general rise in land values. There is, therefore, the attraction to niche developers to extend land holdings to capture some of the growth in capital values which arises from initial enterprise, although this has to be balanced against over commitment to a particular location.

3.9   The general amenity and wider area enhancement of EIPs are in general discounted by niche developers. Their assessments are made on the basis of existing underlying demand, and working within the existing supply factor constraints of the urban fabric. EIPs are seen as useful, but not pre-requisites, although direct grant support, usually in the form of City Grant, is often required. The exception is some of the larger more ambitious area development schemes which are of a scale that significant EIP support - essentially a development subsidy, may be attractive.

Urban renewal developers

3.10 Urban renewal developers' approach concentrates on transforming areas into more attractive environments as a basis for general commercial development. This places the emphasis on comprehensive treatment of the local environment, often involving significant physical or civil engineering inputs by the developer. Developers with civil contracting expertise are concentrated in this group, where capabilities in areas such as land reclamation or infrastructure provision can be applied to advantage.

3.11 Developers in this category are often interested in identifying 'problem' sites where physical treatment will allow development potential to be realised. Importantly, the scale of operations can allow economies and flexibility in development, with the potential to secure uplift in development values as the scheme progresses and the improvements to the area become evident.

3.12 In schemes of this type, developers look to EIPs to include off-site infrastructure such as road access and services. On site, environmental works are incorporated in the main contract and therefore do not lend themselves to separate provision. Advance amenity works are not of particular assistance as these may remove the flexibility of scheme design. Advance infrastructure within EIP's - for example, stabilisation of dock walls or diversion of services, are important as a subsidy to development.

3.13 Urban renewal developers tend to concentrate their activities in Urban Development Corporation and Derelict Land Clearance Areas. Here there is the potential for large scale urban renewal schemes where assistance is available for substantial off-site works and site assembly.

General developers

3.14 General developers have not made urban renewal or inner area projects a specialisation. Many of these developers would avoid regeneration schemes as a matter of course. Particular local knowledge or an historic connection with a site - for example, release from operational use by an associated company, are often the basis for involvement.

3.15 Developers in this category attach more emphasis to EIPs which provide some assurance and support for projects in untested locations and practical evidence of an area's ability to improve its environment.

Development factors and EIPs

3.16 The range of approaches and interests from the different categories of developers suggest that the role and importance of EIPs will reflect the type of the developer, the scale and nature of the scheme involved. We therefore tested this alongside examination of the various development factors identified in Section 2.

3.17 We took the earlier assessment framework (Figure 2.2) and examined the importance of each factor with developers and then reviewed the potential importance of the influence of EIPs in each case, and overall.

3.18 A summary of the views received from developers is given in Figure 3.1. The individual factors are reviewed below. The conclusions and implications are considered subsequently.

Demand factors

Locational and accommodation requirements

3.19 The importance of a clear understanding of potential demand for a scheme in terms of location and accommodation requirements was a constant reference in all developers' comments.

3.20 The emphasis was not only on broad market conditions such as the overall volume and characteristics of potential demand. These are of most relevance to the larger scale urban renewal and general development schemes which might be expected to compete in a wider market. In the case of the smaller scale or free standing projects undertaken by niche or local developers a more detailed consideration of the local demand profile is involved, consistent with the approach of exploiting local market conditions described earlier.

3.21 Developers across all the categories were clear that in general EIPs alone did not significantly influence the overall level and characteristics of property demand across a particular area in terms of location and accommodation requirements, and therefore influence their assessments of these factors.

Environmental requirements

3.22 There was a general recognition that the improvement of an area's environment could assist in influencing demand by creating or reinforcing occupiers' tastes for certain working or living environments. Waterfront environments were a key example, but there were also less specific trends such as the demand for City Centre living. However, physical environment was only one component. Complementary services, leisure and recreation facilities, were identified in some cases as other important components which assisted in presenting balanced working and residential environments. Promoting such a concept is, however, more related to issues of general lifestyle and imaging, rather than simply changing visual perceptions of an area which is examined subsequently.

3.23 Niche developers tended to be more sceptical on this issue. Their predisposition tended to be towards smaller self-contained projects working within the constraints of the existing urban environment rather than seeking to change occupiers' perceptions of their environment.

Figure 3.1 EIP framework: potential impact and developer assessment

Factor	Relative importance	Potential EIP impact	Developer assessment of EIP impact	Comments
Demand Factors				
Locational requirements	●			EIPs not identified as important
Accommodation requirements	●			EIPs not identified as important
Environmental requirements	○	○	●	Urban Renewal and General Development: EIPs can help promote a distinctive location and support investment decisions Niche Developers: not considered relevant to self-contained projects
Economic structure		○		EIP long term effects on economic structure not identified
Availability of public finance		○	○	Limited private sector involvement or understanding of EIP programming
Supply Factors				
Site and premises availability	●	●	●	EIPs site assembly and promotion identified as important
Site access transport and infrastructure	●	●	●	EIP access and service provision identified as important
Quality and characteristics of building and land	●			These factors are not considered important in investment decisions
Surrounding environment	●	●	●	General Developers: area environment seen as an important indicator of investment potential
		●		Urban Renewal Developers; emphasis on EIPs linked to sites,access and services
		●		Niche Developers: quality of area environment not relevant to self-contained projects
Planning and economic policies	○	●	○	Limited perceived integration of planning, economic and EIP programmes
Perception	○			General Developers: reinforced investment decisions
Risk and timing		●		Urban Renewal and Niche Developers: development risk and timing factors unaffected
Profile		●		Urban Renewal Developers: corporate benefits perceived in limited cases
Development viability				
Capital and rental values	○	●	○	Uplift in values associated with improved access and services Improved area amenity may results in swifter letting/sales
Land and development costs	●	●	●	EIP cost subsidy through land reclamation and servicing essential for viability
Note				

● Direct Impact   ○ Indirect Impact

3.24 Urban renewal and general developers were more positive as to the potential, particularly with comprehensive development, for EIPs to assist in creating a distinctive location and environment which could be promoted and stimulate demand to support their investment. However, the role of EIPs was essentially supportive and the lead had to be taken by development investment. Further, the support of EIPs was seen as essentially indirect and beneficial in the longer term, so that the impact of EIPs was identified as weak.

Economic structure

3.25 EIPs alone were not viewed as a significant enough influence to change an industrial area into an office area without the underlying pressures of demand. The longer term economic prospects for an area, for example the progressive replacement of lower value industry by offices, was viewed by developers as an essential function of wider market demand attracted to an area, which might in part be influenced by EIPs.

3.26 Developers interviewed did not take explicit consideration of the local economic structure into account in making development investment decisions. This factor was essentially subsumed in the more immediate considerations of property demand, as expressed in capital and rental values, and property supply in terms of availability and vacancy.

3.27 Most developments are completed over a short timescale whilst changes in local economic structure such as the size and type of businesses, or household income and size are essentially longer term and in any event are more susceptible to wider economic factors than simply improvement in the local environment.

Availability of public finance

3.28 The eligibility of designated inner areas for public sector funding for EIPs was not seen by developers as a material consideration in investment decisions. This reflects the relatively indirect nature of benefits from EIPs as perceived by developers, and the relative lack of contact and co-ordination in this area between public and private sectors in the planning and implementation of projects.

3.29 **Urban Programme:** policies and projects are substantially determined without contact with the private sector. Consultation and grant promotion may take place subsequently, depending on individual schemes, or if the direct participation by the private sector is involved. However, the overall perception and understanding of the Urban Programme across all developer categories is very weak.

3.30 **Derelict Land Grant:** developers were familiar with public and private sector grant regimes. Interaction with the private sector in the promotion of public sector grant schemes was, however, limited. A specific exception is where private sector led schemes are promoted through public sector grant as they are complex or expensive and need the higher levels of grant (100% of eligible costs) available through the public sector regime. All were aware of private sector grant (80% of eligible costs) availability, but the lower level of grant and restrictions on eligible costs were seen to have made this less attractive.

3.31 **Urban Development Corporations:** most developers had a sound understanding of Corporation programmes where they had an interest. Developers involved in larger projects were experienced in working with Urban Development Corporations and were attracted by the range of potential assistance the bodies could offer, of which EIPs were an element. The principal attractions identified were provision of effective transport links and services for the area, land assembly, comprehensive planning and programming and availability of direct grant assistance, principally City Grant.

3.32 Overall, therefore, the linkage between the availability and commitment of public expenditure on EIPs, and development investment was perceived as weak. Developers had little involvement in the planning and programming of works except where receiving direct grant assistance, for example private sector Derelict Land Grant, or in the case of large scale works directly associated with development schemes as in the case of Urban Development Corporations. With a lack of developers' involvement or understanding this must diminish the potential impact of EIPs in terms of short term development perceptions.

Supply Factors

Site and premises availability

3.33 Site assembly is time consuming, involves difficulties and risk working with a range of third parties, and potential inflation of owners' expectations of value. Where planning policy issues remain uncertain this is a further disincentive for developers.

3.34 Developers were positive that where EIPs involved the promotion of development opportunities, and resolution of issues of ownership, planning and services, this strengthened the potential for investment.

3.35 Not only did this approach remove extended time taken in the research of the development options and seeking agreement with owners. Linked to this, EIPs served to assist in reducing developers' risk in the case of reclamation and servicing by taking initial responsibility for these costs.

Site access, transport and infrastructure

3.36 The fundamental requirement for a site to meet the locational requirements of potential occupiers was re-emphasised by developers. EIPs were seen to assist through improvements to site accessability in the immediate environs. Improvements to local roads, separation of pedestrian and vehicle traffic and provision of major services were identified as important in this area.

3.37 The importance of Urban Development Corporations was highlighted because of their role in working in areas which were often poorly served with roads and services and where there was an emphasis in programme budgets on early remedial works.

Quality and characteristics of land and buildings

3.38 Developers were generally sceptical of the importance of EIPs in attracting development investment through simply enhancing the visual qualities of land and buildings. Examples discussed included temporary landscaping, facade improvements to buildings, and planting.

3.39 Developers were doubtful as to whether there were benefits, unless the works related directly to a scheme of development and therefore provided a cost subsidy. Even then, the potential division of contracts was viewed as unattractive. Visual improvement of property in advance of development, beyond safeguarding works to save future cost, was seen as having little value. In essence, the view was that developers were able to identify underlying potential without the assistance of visual improvements to individual sites or buildings.

3.40 However, potential improvements to the general area environment discussed below were viewed more favourably. This may suggest a degree of internal inconsistency with improvements to land and buildings having a role within area improvement, but of little influence on a site specific basis.

Surrounding environment

3.41 Perceptions on the importance of the surrounding environment and the potential impact of EIPs were mixed. Niche developers tended to discount the quality of the surrounding environment and focus on schemes which were essentially self-contained or work within the existing urban fabric. The assistance of EIPs was therefore considered marginal in investment decisions.

3.42 Urban renewal and general developers were more positive as to the requirement of a reasonable standard of environment in an area to encourage investment. Urban renewal developers' emphasis was principally on environmental improvements which provided a physical framework for investment with concentration on highway and services, and also major off-site improvement such as stabilisation of river frontages or dock walls.

3.43 General developers tended to support the view that environment was seen as an important indication of an area's potential for investment and that use of EIPs to promote this is useful. Support from EIPs in strengthening the surrounding environment is seen as important both for physical and visual amenity, but also importantly as a demonstration of commitment to an area.

3.44 Across all categories of developer, however, there was an acceptance that the aspect of the surrounding area will impact on future prospects for development schemes. That is, in the longer term there is an underlying relationship between development investment and environment. Thus whilst the immediate environment in the short term may not be so important as an influence on development investment, the long term potential for improvement and stability of the area generally are important. Where there is the prospect of an areas environment declining then even the most experienced inner area developers will not undertake investment.

Planning and economic policy framework

3.45 The potential linkage between EIPs and wider planning and economic policies was treated by developers with some scepticism. Most developers saw Development Control policies as an important consideration. Few would feel disposed to challenge existing statutory planning policies. The time and cost involved could not be justified for inner area development. Some felt that policies were more susceptible to negotiation as a basis for attracting private investment in areas requiring regeneration.

3.46 Developers were doubtful on the role of development and economic plans as supporting policies linked to action, such as EIPs to assist areas. Reference has been made earlier to the lack of contact and involvement with the private sector at the stage of inception and programming of EIPs. This is reinforced by the perceived lack of integration of planning policies with other regimes such as Urban Programme and Derelict Land Clearance. Urban Development Corporations were the exception with planning policies and funding programmes integrated within their corporate approach.

Perceptions

Risk and timing

3.47 Developers' perceptions as to whether an area's environment influenced assessments of risk and timing of investment reflected the importance they placed on the surrounding environment. This in turn determined the potential importance of EIPs in influencing investment decisions.

3.48 General developers' considerations of risk and timing of investment were most affected by considerations of the surrounding environment, and therefore more potentially most influenced by EIPs. However, the views received were that environmental considerations essentially reinforced investment decisions in terms of perceptions of risk. Other factors, such as demand, location and accessibility were much more important and environmental perceptions did not alter those.

3.49 Environmental perceptions were considered unlikely to alter the timing of investment decisions. In practice, development decisions were taken on the basis of the more important demand and supply factors identified. An enhanced environment through EIPs would help to reinforce investment decisions, but would not significantly alter judgements.

3.50 Urban renewal developers were similarly doubtful as to the impact of environment on their perceptions of risk and timing of investment. Unless EIPs addressed the key factors of access and servicing, changes in an area's visual amenity were seen as of little importance. The larger scale urban renewal projects were in any event designed to create their own environment and to be relatively self contained. Niche developers also tended to take a similar view except that their small scale projects were seen as capable of working within the constraints of prevailing urban environments.

3.51 Whilst the response from developers overall was not particularly positive on the role of EIPs and environment in this context it was accepted that the implementation of works could assist in promoting an area, both to developers and occupiers. Activity, and associated publicity could draw attention to a particular area and raise its profile for occupiers and developers. Urban Development Corporations were seen as particularly effective with their emphasis on corporate promotion. However, this was viewed more as a marketing bonus rather than changing the fundamentals of an area.

Profile

3.52 Across all developer categories the suggestion that commercial judgement would be influenced by association with EIPs and their public agency sponsors was not supported. It was acknowledged by some of the urban renewal developers that there were corporate benefits in an association with the larger higher profile schemes, particularly associated with Urban Development Corporation activity. This had helped to establish their credibility in urban renewal, but it was not their intention to commit themselves to projects which were not soundly based on the principles of demand, location and accessability.

Development viability

Capital and rental values

3.53 Developers interviewed could identify uplifts in capital and rental values where improvements to an area's environment had been the result of improved accessibility or services, or substantive off-site works such as waterfront upgrading linked to specific development projects. In all cases there needs to be a close association between the EIP and development.

3.54 With areas associated with weak property markets this tended to be evidenced in increased sales and lettings rather than uplifts in rental or capital values which were considered longer term benefits. Future potential impacts were heavily discounted as uncertain, and many developers would not necessarily expect to have a continuity of involvement in the area. Where development values rose over the course of longer term schemes this was essentially an addition to profit, commensurate with the scale of the risk and project, and was not included as a factor in the initial investment decision.

Land and development costs

3.55 With area wide improvements being fairly diffuse the potential for identifying cost savings as a consequence of off-site environmental works was difficult for developers to specify. Site specific EIPs, and in particular reclamation, access and service works which contributed directly to offsetting development costs were seen as essential to the viability of many urban regeneration projects. In this context, EIPs were fundamental to the decision to invest.

Developers and EIPs impact on investment

Development investment factors

3.56 The relative importance of individual factors will vary to some extent in each case, but the broad grouping of factors set out in Figure 3.2 reflects the comments of the developers as to their relative importance.

Figure 3.2 Relative Importance of Development Factors

More important factors

Demand	●	Locational requirements
	●	Accommodation requirements
Supply	●	Site and premises availability
	●	Site access, transport and infrastructure
	●	Surrounding environment (general developers)
Development	●	Capital and rental values
viability	●	Land and development costs

Less important factors

Demand	●	Environmental requirements (urban renewal and general developers)
	●	Surrounding environment (urban renewal developers)
Supply	●	Planning and economic policies
Perceptions	●	Risk and timing (general developers)

Unimportant factors

Demand	●	Environmental requirements (niche developers)
	●	Availability of funding for EIP's
Supply	●	Quality and characteristics of buildings and land
perceptions	●	Profile in associating with major schemes

Assessment relates to all groups of developers unless stated.

3.57 In reviewing the importance of investment factors it is possible to identify general themes.

Quantifiable factors: much development investment and decision-taking uses overview judgements based on experience, and supported by an initial financial appraisal which may be refined by further detailed market research. This places a premium on quantifiable factors: demand requirements, capital and rental values, and land and development costs. Non-quantifiable factors such as environment are subsumed in demand and value assessments.

Timescale: financial appraisals tend to be trend based - projecting previous values and assumptions. This tends to reflect the historic position in an area, and discounts future potential for change, for example the impact of environmental improvement.

Direct inputs: the immediate inputs - values and costs are the principal concern in any investment appraisal. This places a premium on grant assistance where the impacts are perceived as most immediate: site costs, and the cost of off-site works, roads and services.

3.58 Developers' assessments of the importance of the environmental context for investment varied according to their experience and the type of schemes with which they were associated.

Niche developers: the orientation towards self-contained projects working with the existing urban fabric, and their experience in inner area markets is reflected in the low importance attached to the considerations of a project's environment.

Urban renewal: the key environmental considerations were linked to the provision of roads, services and the physical framework elements rather than more diffuse amenity works.

General developers: developers who were less specialist in urban renewal development placed greater emphasis on both basic infrastructure and amenity improvements. Whilst improvements to amenity were not seen as important as basic infrastructure, their presence would help to reinforce investment decisions. However, they would not change decisions if other key factors were unsuitable.

EIPs and development investment

3.59 Looking at the developer perceptions where EIPs had an impact, these are concentrated in the supply side factors: site provision, access and infrastructure.

Figure 3.3 Development factors and EIP impact

Important Factors/Significant Impact

Supply	● Site and premises availability
	● Site access transport and infrastructure
	● Surrounding environment (general developers)
Development viability	● Land and development costs

Less important factors/significant impact

Supply	● Surrounding environment (urban renewal developers)

3.60 The relative importance of the amenity of the surrounding environment reflected to a degree on the confidence and experience of the developer working in inner areas, reinforcing rather than changing investment decisions.

3.61 The survey findings are based on general perceptions which may require modification in specific circumstances. However, the broad implications are consistent in their emphasis on supply factors.

3.62 The initial framework which identified the potential for EIP impact has proved rigorous in that no additional EIP impacts on development factors were identified by developers. In some areas where potential for EIP impact was identified, these were found to be weak in practice. In particular the promotion and presentation of EIP's, and their linkages with the presentation of planning and economic policies to the private sector.

Conclusions

3.63 Developers play a central role in urban regeneration, but it is often not a long term commitment and is based on a series of project specific decisions rather than explicit reference to an area's prospects overall. Occupier and longer term investors may be more sensitive to the area's longer term future and the surrounding environment. The format of development appraisal also reinforces tendencies to emphasise the quantifiable and immediate factors and to understate non-quantifiable and longer term factors, such as environmental considerations. Importantly, the value of a stable or improving environment supported by EIPs may be taken for granted. If an area was perceived to be in progressive decline even the more experienced specialist developers would be deterred from committing investment.

Environmental context

3.64 The overall findings of the survey emphasise that the urban environment reflects its economic context, and not the reverse. Sustainable urban regeneration depends on location and accommodation demand in an area. EIPs can remove constraints on an area to allow it to compete, but they cannot create demand. Before EIPs are promoted for economic reasons it follows that there must be a clear understanding of the long term potential of the area and the constraints, which if removed, will allow it to succeed.

Nature of development and developers

3.65 Before the survey we identified three broad categories of developer, and their different qualities and project interests. This has in turn reflected in different attitudes to EIPs so far as the importance of the surrounding environment is concerned.

Niche developers: inner area specialists undertaking freestanding projects with little specific reference to the surrounding environment and limited importance attached to EIPs.

Urban renewal developers: with an emphasis on access, services and infrastructure support as part of EIP programmes.

General developers: attaching importance to access services and infrastructure and also the general quality of the environment as part of EIPs assistance.

3.66 Different types of EIPs will be appropriate depending on the nature of the development projects and the developers involved. In broad terms there appears a pattern and timescale in urban renewal areas:

- starting with smaller scale freestanding projects which are often early initiatives by niche developers

- progressing to provision of a transport infrastructure and services framework for comprehensive urban redevelopment projects by urban renewal specialists

- concluding with amenity improvements to reinforce general developers investment decisions working in an established location.

Nature of EIPs

3.67 Development perceptions of the most effective EIPs are those with the most direct relationship with development. This is evidenced in two contexts:

Financial: where direct grant assistance to developers is perceived as one of the most important EIP impacts on development.

Physical: EIPs with a direct physical relationship to development projects - such as roads and services were seen as more influential.

3.68 In terms of development perceptions therefore the relationship between EIPs and development projects needs to be close to be effective, whether area wide involving a range of sites, or focused on an individual scheme.

Promotion and policy framework

3.69 The relationship between EIPs and the wider planning and economic development framework is seen as weak for the most part. Outside Urban Development Corporations, EIPs appear to present a picture of one-off projects rather than having an overall relationship with general area or site policy. This appears to reflect a number of factors:

- relatively little involvement of the private sector in preparation and planning of EIP programmes

- weak perceived linkage between planning and economic policies and EIP programming

- promotion of EIP projects can be weak.

3.70 Overall, the developers' survey suggests that EIPs, promoted for economic regeneration can affect investment attitudes and perceptions, and that there may be a tendency to understate their impact. However, EIPs effectiveness depends on:

- the area or sites' economic context and potential

- the requirements of the development and the extent to which it is dependent on its environment and context

- the requirements of the developer as to the importance placed on environment, site access, transport and infrastructure

- the direct relationship of EIPs to development, through grants to developers, and site related improvements such as roads and services

- improved promotion, effective integration with other policy programmes and consultation with the private sector.

4 Case study framework

EIP case study assessment framework

4.1   This section sets out the basis for case study selection and assessment. The same assessment framework has been used as earlier to examine the potential for impact of EIPs on development investment factors in Section 2, and subsequently tested in the developers' survey. This has been applied to some thirty case studies to identify the important factors which influence private sector investment.

4.2   Taking each of the development factors we have identified the broad features of EIPs associated with each in Figure 4.1, together with examples. In assessing each of the case studies we have identified the prominent EIP features and their contribution. The features identified in the framework are broad in their application and in practice overlap.

Figure 4.1 Development Factors and EIP Features

Development Factor	EIP Features	Examples of Features
Demand		
Locational requirements	Area assessment	Property, economic and environmental assessments of project area
Accommodation requirements		
Environmental requirements		
Economic structure		
Availability of public finance	Promotion and consultation	Marketing, newsletter, public consultation
Supply		
Site and premises availability	Development	Site assembly, development briefs, direct development
Site access transport & infrastructure	Highways and infrastructure	Road improvements, pedestrianisation, parking, services
Quality and characteristics of buildings & land	Property rehabilitation	Facade improvements, site landscaping
Surrounding environment	Amenity Improvements	Public open space, walkways, lighting
Planning and economic policies	Policy linkage	Integration of planning, economic and development policies and programmes, planning briefs
Perception		
Risk and timing	Promotion and consultation	Development partnership, consultation
Profile	Partnership	Development partnership and informal associations
Development Viability		
Capital and Rental Values		
Land and Development Costs	Grant assistance	Land clearance, servicing, building cleaning and repair

4.3 This framework is not designed to be exclusive and in applying this to case studies we have also provided for the identification of other features which have been important in the impact of EIPs.

Case study selection

4.4 The case studies were selected to give evidence of best practice where projects had been successful. The case study areas were divided between the three regimes included in this study and taken from six regions. The projects were selected in each of the areas in consultation with the DoE Regional Office and Local Authorities. The case studies are listed in Figures 4.2 and 4.3.

Figure 4.2 EIP Case Studies: Area Programmes

Project	Type	Programme	Expenditure £m (Approved)	Timescale
New Ferry, Wirral	Retail: inner area	Urban Programme	1.36	1985-89
Hyson Green, Nottingham	Retail: inner area	Urban Programme	0.41 (0.55)	1982-
Lace Market, Nottingham	Commercial: city centre	Urban Programme	10.10 (*)	1979-
Mathew Street, Liverpool	Commercial: city centre	Urban Programme	0.90 (1.45) (*)	1979-
New Basford, Nottingham	Commercial: inner area	Urban Programme	0.76 (*)	1982-
Ouseburn, Newcastle	Commercial: inner area	Urban Programme	1.47 (*)	1977-
Stoney Lane, Rainhill, Merseyside	Commercial: inner area	Urban Programme	0.02	1988
Whitworth Street, Manchester	Residential: city centre	Urban Development Corporation	0.99	1991-
Greater Manchester Museum of Science and Technology	Leisure and amenity: city centre	Urban Development Corporation	0.24	1989
Closegate, Newcastle	Leisure and amenity: city centre	Urban Development Corporation	3.86	1988-91
Blackbrook Valley, Dudley	Leisure and amenity: inner area	Derelict Land Grant	0.13	1982-
Watery Lane, Walsall	Leisure and amenity inner area	Derelict Land Grant	0.19	1984-90
North Shields & Fish Quay, Tyneside	Mixed use: inner area	Urban Development Corporation	3.41	1988-91
Nottingham & Beeston Canal, Nottingham	Mixed Use: inner area	Urban Programme	0.23	1981-90
Castlefield, Manchester	Mixed Use: inner area	Urban Development	2.75	1989-

Note: ( ) approved budget
(*) includes other grant expenditure
(**) net cost after sale proceeds

Figure 4.3 EIP Case Studies: Site Projects

Project	Type	Programme	Expenditure £m (Approved)	Timescale
Gerard Gamble Building, Nottingham	Commercial: rehabilitation	Urban Programme	1.11 (*)	1980, 1990-
Daisyfield Mill, Blackburn	Commercial: rehabilitation	Derelict Land Grant	0.05	1986-91
South SeftonBC, Bootle	Commercial: rehabilitation	Urban Programme	0.45	1989-91
Qualcast Site, Wolverhampton	Commercial: under 10 acres	Derelict Land Grant	0.41	1983-90
Bentley Site, Walsall	Commercial: under 10 acres	Derelict Land Grant	0.55	1983-89
Newhalley, Rawtenstall	Commercial: over 10 acres	Derelict Land Grant	0.60 (**)	1985-90
GEC Site, Clayton le Moors	Commercial: over 10 acres	Derelict Land Grant	0.70	1984-86
Westwood Power Station, Wigan	Commercial: over 10 acres	Derelict Land Grant	0.09 (**)(1.2)	1987-
Black Lake, West Bromwich	Residential: under 10 acres	Derelict Land Grant	0.45	1987-89
Blakeley Hall, West Bromwich	Residential: under 10 acres	Derelict Land Grant	0.08	1985-88
Chad Road, Bamford	Residential: under 10 acres	Derelict Land Grant	1.26 (***)	1985-89
Towneley Brickworks, Burnley	Residential: over 10 acres	Derelict Land Grant	0.32	1988-91
Moseley Common, Wigan	Residential: over 10 acres	Derelict Land Grant	1.24	1987-91
St Peters Marina, Newcastle	Residential: over 10 acres	Urban Development Corporation	11.61	1988-91
St Peters Riverside, Sunderland	Residential: over 10 acres	Urban Development Corporation	6.7 (27)	1988-

Note: ( ) approved budget   (*) includes other grant expenditure
(**) net cost after sale proceeds (***) estimated

Area projects and site projects

4.5   The projects almost exclusively focus on private sector development, but in three cases either public agencies or the Local Authority has been the developer, acting as a catalyst, where prevailing market conditions remain unable to support private sector development.

4.6   The EIP case studies have been divided between:

- area wide (Section 5)

- site specific (Section 6).

4.7   We have adopted this classification, both to assist case study arrangement, and to examine whether differences can be identified in the implications of either approach.

Project type

4.8   Under each heading we have grouped the projects according to their principal use to see if this has implications for the effectiveness of EIPs. Where possible we have also tested a secondary characteristic (location, size, rehabilitation or development). However, the size of the case study sample, and the individual circumstances affecting each project, place limits on this exercise.

Programmes

4.9   The programmes under which EIPs were undertaken are identified. In somecases a mix of programmes was used and the lead programme is identified here. For example certain Derelict Land Grant projects may have also been located in Urban Development Corporation Areas. A broadly equal representation of projects from each programme is examined.

Expenditure

4.10 The project expenditure to date is shown, with total expenditure approval shown in brackets for continuing projects, where this is known. Where this includes significant elements of other programme expenditure this is noted. The details are given in the full case study, but typically this includes one of the following:

- Local Authority Capital Programmes

- English Heritage (Town Schemes)

- European Regional Development Fund

- Countryside Commission.

Capital returns, for example from land sales, have not been deducted except where net expenditure information was only available.

4.11 City Grant (or Urban Development Grant) expenditure is not included in these figures as this is applied as a direct development subsidy, without reference to environmental considerations. However, this expenditure is identified in the case studies.

4.12 The range of project expenditure is very large, indicative of the varied applications of EIPs:

- Urban Programme: £0.02m - £10.1 million (*)

- Derelict Land Grant: £0.05m - £1.43 million

- Urban Development Corporation: £0.24m - £11.61 million

    *   includes some non-urban programme funding.

Timescale

4.13 The timescale of the projects is given from programme planning to completion. The range of timescales of the projects is as follows:

- **Urban Programme:** a feature is the extended timescale with programmes frequently running over 10 years

- **Derelict Land Grant:** up to 10 years in one case which is a programme comprising a number of individual schemes. Individual projects are completed inside four years.

- **Urban Development Corporations:** some projects have been running for over four years since the inception of the UDC area, but is is a feature of the UDC areas selected that they are relatively early in the lifetime of their programme.

The longer running projects tend to comprise a continuing programme of expenditure on a collection of smaller projects.

The following sections examine the individual projects.

5 Case studies: area programmes

5.1   This section examines a selection of area programme Environmental Improvement Projects, their key features and impacts in relation to economic objectives and concludes with a review of the area programme case studies. This provides a basis for examining the overall findings of the impact of EIPs on urban regeneration in Section 7. In each case we have provided a project summary and outlined the important EIP features.

Area programmes   5.2   Area based programmes provide a framework for a group of projects or individual projects with an area wide application. The programmes have two sets of objectives.

> **Programme objectives:** typically broad policy objectives of urban regeneration and economic development. The case studies selected all achieved their general programme objectives, although the level of success varied and in many cases the programmes were seen as continuing.

> **Project objectives:** the immediate objectives of land reclamation, building rehabilitation and so on were all achieved. The final objectives, economic regeneration and the attraction of private investment have been examined in each case in seeking to identify the successful features in each case.

5.3   The case studies are divided between the following categories:

- Retail: Inner area

- Commercial: City centre and inner area

- Residential: City centre

- Leisure and Amenity: City centre and inner area

- Mixed use: Inner area

Figure 5.1 Case Studies: Area Programme Features

Project	Area assessment	Promotion consultation	Development	Highways infrastructure	Property rehabilitation	Amenity improvement	Policy linkage	Partnership	Grant assistance	Other features
Retail: inner area										
New Ferry, Wirral	●	●	●	●	●	●			●	Programming timescale
Hyson Green, Nottingham		●	●	●		●			●	
Commercial: city centre										
Lace Market, Nottingham	●	●	●	●	●	●	●	●	●	Programming timescale
Mathew St, Liverpool	●	●	●	●	●	●	●		●	Funding mixture
Commercial: inner area										
New Basford, Nottingham	●	●	●	●	●				●	Funding mixture
Ouseburn, Newcastle	●	●	●	●	●	●			●	
Stoney Lane, Rainhill		●		●						
Residential: city centre										
Whitworth St, Manchester	●	●	●		●	●	●			Funding mixture
Leisure: city centre										
Great Manchester Museum of Science	●					●	●			
Closegate, Newcastle	●	●	●	●		●				
Leisure: Inner Area										
Blackbrook Valley, Dudley				●	●					
Watery Lane, Walsall				●	●					
Mixed Use: Inner Area										
North Shields and Fish Quay, Tyneside	●	●	●	●	●	●	●		●	Grant mixing
Nottingham and Beeston Canal, Nottingham	●	●	●	●			●	●	●	
Castlefield, Manchester	●	●	●	●		●			●	

Casework study 1
New Ferry, Wirral

Urban Programme   Time: 1985-89
Inner area district centre renewal   Expenditure:£1.3 million

Features

- Area Assessment   ● Promotion   ● Development
- Highways and Infrastructure   ● Property Rehabilitation
- Amenity Improvements   ● Grant Assistance
- Other Factors: Programming, Timescale

5.4   New Ferry is an inner area district centre which had not adapted to the contemporary pressures of town centre and out of centre retailing. The centre's layout reflected an historic, extended, linear arrangement comprising an excess of small units dominated by independent traders and a progressive loss of remaining multiple traders. Increasing vacancy and dereliction were cumulatively eroding the stability and function of the centre with consequent physical decay, loss of services and damage to the local economy.

5.5   The project has involved the preparation of a comprehensive area improvement programme comprising highway diversion, pedestrianisation, redevelopment and grant assisted property improvements. This has been supported by more general amenity works. The Local Authority has undertaken extensive consultation and promotion of the scheme.

5.6   The New Ferry scheme has substantially achieved its objectives over a four year period. Decline has been arrested and the environment improved. Retailers have invested in their own premises through property acquisition and improvement. The vacancy rate for the retail units has dropped from 17% to under 2%. The development of a supermarket in scale with the existing retail structure will reinforce the centre's function. The establishment of a pedestrianised area has provided a physical framework for the environmental improvements.

Features

Area assessment: in preparing the area programme the Local Authority undertook an assessment of the function, economic potential, and environment of the area. This informed decisions to consolidate extended retail frontages, revise traffic circulation, and assemble land for supermarket development. It has been important in achieving programme co-ordination, direction and momentum.

Promotion and consultation: the Local Authority undertook extensive consultation and promotion of the programme including newsletters and on-site representation. This has helped to involve property owners and occupiers and promote grant take-up and investment.

Development: site clearance and assembly were undertaken by Local Authority for supermarket development. Without this initiative it is very unlikely that the supermarket operator would have pursued its interest. The supermarket provides an important anchor for the District Centre's function.

Highways and infrastructure: through traffic was diverted with pedestrianisation and new car parking area. This has radically changed the retail environment, improving accessibility for pedestrians and car borne shoppers.

Property rehabilitation: an extensive external building improvements programme has combined the application of enveloping schemes with grants for shop frontages, targeted at key locations.

Amenity improvements: limited improvements adjoining public open space have been made, together with landscaping to car parking areas and improvement of the perimeter.

Grant assistance: grants for shop front improvement (up to 80% of eligible costs) have been promoted successfully, combining targeted application to key frontages with effective promotion and consultation to achieve a high take-up.

Programming: the New Ferry scheme has followed a clear phased programme of projects from inception to completion providing momentum and a focus for objectives and effort.

Timescale: the programme was completed in four years, a reflection of the initial programming and focused resources. Implementation of programmes and resources have therefore been closely linked to achieve maximum impact.

Case study 2

Hyson Green, Nottingham

Urban programme   Time: 1982-91
Inner area district centre renewal   Expenditure: £1.3 million

Features

- Area assessment
- Highways and infrastructure
- Amenity improvements
- Other factors: programming and timescale

- Promotion

- Development
- Property rehabilitation
- Grant assistance

5.7   Hyson Green is an inner area district centre with extended retail frontages along the local major roads. The property stock was dominated by small retail units with a pattern of increasing vacancy and demolition, and a consequent loss of retail function. The area is affected by poor social conditions and prostitution.

5.8   The principal actions of the Local Authority have been grant assistance for improvement to shop frontages, demolition of council high rise flats and site redevelopment for a superstore, together with footpath and public open space works. The Shopping Centre was designated a Central Improvement Area in 1989, but Urban Programme assistance to the area began in 1982.

5.9   The Hyson Green scheme has achieved improvements to the environment and arrested progressive decline. However, the local economy is very depressed and the longer term underlying economic improvement of the area remains to be achieved. The vacancy rate for retail units remains around 20%. The anticipated wider trading benefits of a superstore development in the centre have not yet materialised. The timescale of the project has been extended whilst the centre has yet to establish itself at a level which will allow sustainable trading.

Features

Promotion: this has been intermittent and linked to promotion of improvement grants to shop frontages. This has encouraged grant take-up, but the overall momentum has been weak.

Development: the site available after clearance of the former council housing block has been sold to Asda and developed as a superstore. This has demonstrated commitment to the area, but it is questionable whether the scale and form of superstore retailing complement retail functions of the District Centre.

Highways and infrastructure: footpath improvements have been undertaken. These have improved the pedestrian environment, but the problem of significant levels of traffic passing through the area remains.

Amenity improvements: there have been limited improvements to public open space which have contributed to the general amenity of the area.

Grant assistance: grant assistance has been made available to shop owners for frontage improvements. This assistance, however, has been general in application leading to fragmented improvement.

Programming: the Hyson Green scheme has evolved over time through a series of successive projects which has not provided the focus and momentum which a clear phased programme might have provided, accepting that local conditions are adverse.

Timescale: the Hyson Green scheme has run over 10 years in various forms, a reflection of the extended programming which has evolved.

Commercial projects: (city centre)

Case Study 3

Lace Market, Nottingham

Urban Programme

Inner area commercial area renewal
(including other programmes)

Time: 1979-

Expenditure: £10.1 million

Features

- Area assessment
- Development
- Property rehabilitation
- Policy linkage
- Grant assistance
- Programming
- Promotion and consultation
- Highways and infrastructure
- Amenity improvement
- Partnership
- Timescale
- Funding mixture

5.10 The Lace Market is a unique area of eighteenth and nineteenth century buildings in Nottingham, close to the City Centre and with a long association with the textile industry. The area is dominated by multi-storey warehouses and factories extending over 30hectares approximately, with both derelict areas and neglected buildings. A central aim has been the retention of textile manufacturing in this location.

5.11 The City Council initially established a comprehensive area plan in 1969 using Conservation Area powers and subsequently the area was designated an Industrial Improvement Area in 1979. These have provided the framework for grant assistance, block and facelift improvements, together with parking provision, and public and private sector development. The latest initiative is a joint public:private sector development company for the area.

5.12 The Lace Market project has been very successful with over 30 derelict sites and nearly 200 buildings treated, some 650,000 ft^2 office floorspace and 3 residential projects created. The project in its various forms has now been in operation for over 20 years, and has successfully turned around an area of neglect where expectations were low. Two major environmental awards have been given to schemes in the area. The local employment base has diversified and stabilised. Development, however, continues to require grant support and is not self sustaining. This is a reflection of market conditions and in some cases difficult site conditions.

Features

Area assessment: the Lace Market has been the subject of successive assessments and a series of comprehensive development plans since its inception. These have provided a framework for activities, but succeeding plans and modifications may have eroded some of the promotion and momentum for the area.

Promotion and consultation: the area programme has been extensively promoted using Conservation Area, Industrial Improvement Area and Town Scheme powers, together with consultations with owners and occupiers. However, promotion has not been continuous and changes in programme formats may not have assisted momentum.

Development: the City Council has been responsible for assembling and providing development opportunities and clearing sites. Private development projects have been promoted with grant assistance, together with the City Council undertaking redevelopment of its own property, and forming a joint venture development company with private interests. These have all been positive features. The use of Development Control policies in the past to exclude office use and protect existing industrial use may have suppressed potential growth in values to assist development viability, and encouraged owners to postpone schemes in the hope of securing office use at a later date. However, since changes in the Planning Use Classes in 1987 such constraints have not existed.

Highways and Infrastructure: pedestrianisation and car parking schemes have been implemented which have made a significant contribution to pedestrian and car accessibility.

Property Rehabilitation: grants for external repair and building cleaning have been provided, and enforcement of repair conditions of Council property. However, such assistance cannot tackle problems of structural repair or modernisation often required in older properties.

Amenity Improvements: open space and landscaping provision have been included in the programme. These have been integrated with highway and development projects to provide mutual support and encourage a critical mass of development.

Policy Linkage: planning, economic and development policy have been co-ordinated particularly in using Town Scheme and Conservation Area control and in subsidised development to assist the indigenous textile industry.

Partnership: a joint venture development company with private sector interests has been created to undertake projects. This has assisted in diversifying funding sources for further development.

Grant Assistance: a range of EIP grant assistance has been provided direct for development. This has provided financial support essential for significant private sector investment in a relatively weak local property market.

Programming: the concentration of resources on the Lace Market has been sustained. As such the evolution of changing programmes and there revision over time has to a degree been offset through sustained action and funding.

Timescale: the timescale of the project has now extended over 20 years in various forms, with Urban Programme involved over 10 years, which is in part a reflection of the extension to the Lace Market programme area.

Funding Mixture: the project has successfully tapped a wide range of funding in addition to Urban Programme including English Heritage and Council Capital Programme as well as projects attracting Urban Development Grant. This has allowed a diversity of funding and objectives to be met.

Case study 4

Mathew Street, Liverpool

Urban Programme
City centre retail and office area renewal

Time: 1979-
Expenditure: £0.9 million
(£1.45 million programmed)

Features

- Area assessment
- Development
- Property rehabilitation
- Grant assistance

- Promotion and consultation
- Highways and infrastructure
- Policy linkage
- Funding mixture

5.13   The Mathew Street area is located between Liverpool's retail core and central business district. It is occupied by a mixture of eighteenth and nineteenth century warehouses and office buildings and extends over 9 hectares approximately. Many of the buildings in the area were in very poor condition and vacant, and the area was experiencing significant decline.

5.14   The City Council established a comprehensive area framework using Conservation Area powers. This provided the planning framework for environmental works using Urban Programme, including pedestrianisation, facade facelifts and grants for repairs. The City Council also successfully promoted a major specialist retail and office scheme (Cavern Walks) in the centre of the area, developed by the private sector with grant assistance.

5.15   The Mathew Street area initiative has successfully supported the refurbishment of buildings to provide a mixture of specialist shopping, restaurants and other services together with offices. In addition, a major specialist retail and office development (Cavern Walks: 95,650ft^2 net) has been undertaken in the area. Instead of remaining a marginal location, the location has effectively provided a link between the City Centre retail and office areas.

Features

Area assessment: the use of Conservation Area powers has successfully provided a framework for improvement. The designation involved a careful assessment of property, economic and environmental potential. This was taken forward in Town Scheme programming.

Promotion and consultation: this has been intermittent, depending on resources. Contacting property owners has proved difficult and time consuming whilst co-operation in repair grants and initiatives has not always been forthcoming. As a consequence, momentum and the perceptions of the overall strategy on the area have been lost to a degree.

Development: the promotion of Cavern Walks for retail and office development has secured substantial private sector investment, although the trading location is not sufficiently strong to support extensive retail development and this element of the scheme has not traded particularly well. More generally, smaller scale refurbishment and investment by owner occupiers has provided a stable private investment base although there are prominent buildings which remain derelict.

Highways and infrastructure: the area has been pedestrianised with restricted service access. This has improved the visual amenity of the area but servicing and parking remain intrusive. To allow improved security in the evenings parking has been re-admitted.

Property rehabilitation: grants have been made available for external repairs (up to 40% eligible expenditure). Where some of the buildings now require structural repair and internal re-organisation the value for money in the longer term is uncertain.

Policy linkage: environmental improvements have been linked to planning policy controls under Conservation Area and Town Scheme programmes. This has allowed Development Control powers to be exercised in association with external improvement grants.

Grant assistance: grants have been made available for external repair works (up to 40% of eligible costs) to properties. The relatively modest level of grants and the approval procedures, although kept simple, have acted as disincentives in some cases.

Programming: the projects have been implemented incrementally without an overall programme, but concentrated within a relatively small area which has provided a sense of momentum.

Commercial projects: (Inner area)

Case study 5

New Basford, Nottingham

Urban programme
Inner area industrial area renewal

Time: 1982-
Expenditure: £0.76 million
(including other grant sources)

Features

- Area assessment
- Development
- Highways and infrastructure
- Grant assistance

- Promotion and consultation
- Property rehabilitation
- Amenity improvements
- Grant mixing

5.16 New Basford is a traditional inner industrial area containing a large number of Victorian multi-storey industrial properties, together with pockets of housing. In the early 1980s, with the decline of traditional manufacturing industry, the area was showing substantial evidence of decay when the Council declared it an Industrial Improvement Area. Most recently, Shipstone's brewery, the major business of the area, vacated its premises.

5.17 Some four years after IIA designation the Council prepared an area development strategy as a framework for action. This has included industrial improvement grants, amenity works, access improvements, and acquisition and redevelopment of key sites.

5.18 The New Basford project has been very successful. Environmental decay has been tackled, redevelopment and refurbishment of buildings by the private sector has taken place, with floorspace take-up increased, and rental levels strong. The swift re-occupation of the former Shipstone's brewery has assisted continuing momentum of the area.

Features

Area assessment: a comprehensive area assessment and strategy was prepared, although this was delayed in its inception. The initial IIA designation was more of a vehicle for grant assistance than planned area renewal.

Promotion and consultation: the Council has approached building owners direct to consult and promote grant take-up as well as co-ordinating an advertising campaign. This has increased the awareness of area improvements and the grant assistance available.

Development: the Council has acquired, cleared and sold, two prominent sites for development using Derelict Land Grant powers. This has assisted in promoting the momentum for renewal in the area.

Highways and infrastructure: access and off-street car parking improvements have been completed which have provided an improved working environment and traffic control.

Property rehabilitation: grants have been provided for building rehabilitation through IIA provision and these have been taken up by owners.

Amenity improvements: small scale clearance, landscaping and tree planting have been undertaken. These projects have been linked to the more substantial works such as clearance for redevelopment and highways and parking improvements.

Grant assistance: grant funding has been provided under IIA powers.

Funding mixture: in addition to Urban Programme, Derelict Land Grant has been used, and City Grant attracted to a neighbouring scheme.

Case Study 6

Ouseburn, Newcastle

Urban Programme
Inner area industrial area renewal

Time: 1977-
Expenditure: £1.47 million
(including other grant sources)

Features

- Area Assessment
- Highways and Infrastructure
- Amenity Improvements

- Development
- Property Rehabilitation
- Grant Assistance

5.19 Ouseburn Valley is located at the bottom of a ravine crossed by viaducts and with poor road access. The area is dominated by substantial Victorian buildings and extends over 20 hectares. The project has faced substantial problems with a weak local economy and physical constraints. The scheme started with the objective of arresting decline. In this sense it has been successful, with a significant improvement in the local environment which is recognised by local businesses. Private sector investment has not as yet been attracted to the area, but there are early signs of interest with the prospect of riverside improvements and potential development of adjoining quayside areas.

5.20 Since original designation in 1977, the project area has been progressively extended. Initially designation was an enabling exercise to provide access to grant funding to support individual projects, with the attraction of private investment a later priority after safeguarding of existing business. In 1988, an area based development strategy was instituted. The range of projects completed includes environmental works, road improvements and development by the Council. Development schemes from the private sector are now at the proposal stage, using City Grant and Derelict Land Grant.

Features

Area assessment: an area based strategy has now been applied to provide a comprehensive framework for action.

Development: site clearance and development has been through the Council to date, but there are early signs of private sector investment.

Highways and infrastructure: access and road improvements have assisted the area, and the prospect of waterfront improvement incorporating a barrage has attracted private sector interest to the area.

Property rehabilitation: this has principally involved the Council refurbishing a warehouse as an arts and studio complex, and limited take-up of grants by local occupiers.

Amenity improvement: the focus of much of the action to date has been a wide range of small scale amenity works. The longer term proposal to dam the river and raise the water level is attracting potential interest in the area from developers.

Grant assistance: limited grants have been made available under IIA powers for property improvement.

Case Study 7

Stoney Lane, Rainhill, Merseyside

Urban Programme
Inner and industrial area renewal

Time: 1988
Expenditure: £0.02 million

Features

- Highways and infrastructure

5.21 Stoney Lane Industrial Estate is a local estate containing a small number of owner occupiers with Council owned land to the rear. The Council acquired, upgraded and adopted the service road to release the development potential of its land and attracted new investment to the estate.

Features

Highways and infrastructure: the improved estate road was essential to new company investment on the estate and also supported additional development demand for the Council's land holding.

Residential projects: city centre

Casework study 8

Whitworth Street, Manchester

Urban Development Corporation
City centre residential renewal area

Time: 1991
Expenditure: £0.99 million

Features

- Area assessment
- Amenity improvement
- Property rehabilitation
- Promotion
- Grant mixing

5.22 Whitworth Street is unique amongst the case studies as an area environmental improvement project which is focused on residential development. The area is one of the six key areas identified in the Central Manchester Development Corporation Plan. It is characterised by imposing four and five storey warehouse buildings which were in decay. The Development Corporation's strategy is to support the development of the area for residential use creating a 'village in the city'.

5.23 The project has adopted a number of established inner area improvement measures including facade cleaning, street lighting, footpath improvements and floodlighting.

5.24 The environmental projects have just commenced with completion due over the next couple of years at a total cost of £1 million. The impact at this stage is difficult to determine. Certainly, some benefits were anticipated by developers who have taken the view that the area would improve following the designation of the Urban Development Corporation. However, it is clear that the availability of City Grant funding, and the demonstration effect of certain early development schemes have been influential factors.

5.25 There are now three residential development schemes completed with a total value of £10.5 million together with two hotels and a further two residential and commercial schemes being progressed. Initial sales of flats have been slow but this is seen as a reflection of prevailing economic circumstances and the developers are convinced of the long term potential of the area.

Features

Area assessment: the projects follow an earlier property, economic and environmental assessment of the area undertaken as part of the Urban Development Corporation's initial plan.

Promotion: the implementation of the improvements has been extensively publicised by the Urban Development Corporation. Developers confirm that the involvement of the Urban Development Corporation has raised the profile and the interest in the area.

Development: the improvements have been linked to the development opportunities identified by the Urban Development Corporation and promoted to housebuilders.

Property rehabilitation: the emphasis has been on the retention and conversion of warehouse buildings for flats. Facade cleaning and street lighting projects have been instituted to help improve the attraction of the area.

Amenity improvement: facade cleaning, street lighting, floodlighting and footpath improvements have been implemented and in some cases involving contributions from building owners. At this stage, developers have not placed much emphasis on the impact of these improvements.

Policy linkage: the improvements form part of the Urban Development Corporation's overall strategic plan.

Grant mixing: the development projects have attracted City Grant support in addition to Urban Development Corporation expenditure in the area. Direct grant has been critical in attracting private sector investment.

Leisure and amenity

Casework Study 9

Greater Manchester Museum of Science and Technology

Urban Development Corporation	Time:	1989
Leisure area amenity works	Expenditure:	£0.24million

Features

- Area assessment
- Amenity improvement

5.26 GMMSI was a focus for part of Central Manchester Development Corporation's environmental work programme. Its purpose is to act as a catalyst for the surrounding Castlefield area and to enhance the area's leisure and tourism potential. The works involved building repair, lighting, exhibitions and clearance of redundant buildings at a cost of £0.24 million.

5.27 GMMSI's improvements form part of an overall programme of improvements to the Castlefield area. The individual works described are relatively modest. They have reinforced perceptions that the area is improving as a location for private sector investment, and may have helped support the growing attendance at GMMSI. Developers responsible for hotel and leisure projects in the area remain of the opinion that it is the location and attraction of the individual projects that is important, rather than their inter-relationship and links with the area. The impacts of improvements have been limited at this stage and are only likely to be seen in the longer term, providing a framework for future development rather than supporting existing projects.

Features

Area assessment: the environmental works followed a comprehensive property, economic and environmental assessment of the area but the Urban Development Corporation.

Amenity improvements: the improvements enhanced the immediate environment of the museum but were not specifically linked to other development projects. The overall benefit of the improvements is at best uncertain at this stage.

Casework Study 10

Closegate, Newcastle

Urban Development Corporation Inner area public open space	Time: Expenditure:	1988-91 £3.86million

Features

- Area assessment
- Amenity improvement
- Funding mixture

- Highways and infrastructure
- Development
- Grants

5.28 Closegate was an ambitious flagship project of the Tyne & Wear Development Corporation involving the redevelopment of a derelict escarpment to provide Hanging Gardens as a focus for the environmental improvement and regeneration of the area. This was linked to highway improvements and a riverside walkway. The cost of the programme of works was some £3.9million, with further input from City Grant towards associated hotel and potential office developments.

5.29 The scheme has been successful in creating an effective link with the City Centre and providing a prominent environmental statement. The project is linked to a major quality hotel development (4 star: 156 bedrooms) which has been complemented by a proposed office scheme (75,000 ft²), which is awaiting pre-letting. In addition, proposals for further commercial development in the area have now been promoted. The scheme has supported the hotel project, although it was not a prerequisite for the development. The creation of a high quality public open area adjoining existing buildings and development has significantly enhanced the visual amenity of the location and provided an effective use for land incapable of physical development.

Features

Area assessment: the Closegate scheme forms part of the Urban Development Corporation's integrated plan for the area involving highways, waterfrontage improvements, and development.

Highways and infrastructure: an important element of the area scheme was the improvement of highways and the separation of pedestrians with the development of a riverside walkway.

Development: the Urban Development Corporation were responsible for the acquisition and clearance of the hotel and office site which were essential to attract development.

Amenity improvement: the removal of dereliction and the creation of an attractive feature of a prominent derelict site with a pedestrian link to the City Centre has made an important contribution to the area, but were not a pre-requisite for the hotel development.

Funding mixture: City Grant has been essential for the development of the hotel.

Leisure & amenity: (inner area)

Casework Study 11

Blackbrook Valley, Dudley

| Derelict Land Grant | Time: | 1982- |
| Reclamation of derelict open area for public recreation | Expenditure: | £0.13 million |

Features

- Amenity improvement
- Property rehabilitation

5.30 Blackbrook Valley forms part of an industrial corridor extending for a mile between Netherton and the Merry Hill retail and commercial area. The Valley is an open area of some 60 acres, containing extensive mine workings, tailings and landfill. The boundaries adjoin established industrial areas of Brierley Hill, Saltwells and Netherton. The site provides strategic amenity and public open space in which has been established a Nature Reserve and Site of Special Scientific Interest. The land has been progressively reclaimed over the last nine years.

5.31 The impact of Blackbrook Valley reclamation on adjoining commercial development areas is difficult to assess. Developers, agents and occupiers in the area believe that environmental improvements were desirable, whilst the Enterprise

Zone development incentives were of greater importance. With the removal of Development Control restrictions in the Enterprise Zone it is evident that some of the development currently taking place in the designated EZ area has little reference to the Blackbrook Valley reclamation which it borders. Attempts by the Local Authority to provide design guidance have not been supported by developers. Some schemes in the area such as the Blackbrook Business Park have included landscaping within the development to good effect.

Features

Amenity improvement: the principal feature of the project has been the removal of a major derelict site. This has been supported by developers and occupiers in the area. However, in attracting investment the developers major concerns are focused on EZ incentives, and the need for improved highways to serve business.

Property improvement: the reclamation of the land has improved the surrounding area and its environmental quality. The impact on investment in the surrounding industrial area is seen as modest, but part of a longer term process of area improvement.

Casework study 12

Watery Lane, Walsall

Derelict Land Grant	Time:	1984-90
Reclamation of derelict open area for public recreation	Expenditure:	£0.19 million

Features

● Amenity improvement   ● Property rehabilitation

5.32 Watery Lane was formerly a site for colliery spoil and sandpit working extending over 17 acres. It lies between Willenhall and Neachell and provides a buffer between residential and industrial areas. The scheme has provided the focus for two residential schemes in the immediate vicinity and also attracts recreational users. The project has been unable to incorporate an adjoining scrap yard because of its high existing use value. Notwithstanding this, the environment has improved sufficiently to support adjoining residential development which looks out onto the reclaimed area.

Features

Amenity improvement: the scheme has successfully removed derelictworkings and provided a visual focus for development in the area, despite bad neighbour uses remaining in the immediate vicinity.

Property rehabilitation: the reclamation of the site has improved the area's environs and demonstrated the potential to provide an attractive environment. This has re-inforced residential development perceptions and investment as to the future prospects of the area.

Mixed use (inner area)

Casework study 13

North Shields and Fish Quay, Tyneside

Urban Development Corporation
Area renewal to support fishing and
indigenous industries and tourism

Time: 1988-91
Expenditure: £3.41 million

Features

- Area assessment
- Development
- Property rehabilitation
- Grant assistance

- Promotion and consultation
- Highways and infrastructure
- Policy linkage
- Funding mixture

5.33 North Shields Riverside is an area based environmental programme funded through the Tyne and Wear Development Corporation and addressing the Tyne waterfront and fish quay area. The project has sought to integrate groupings of small scale environmental improvements and link these with wider economic objectives. A key aim is to provide assistance to the shore based activities of the local fishing industry and to diversify the local economic base through tourism development. In addition, there has been support for residential and commercial development in the waterfront area. Project implementation began in 1988 with small scale improvements, and has progressed to larger scale quayside works in 1990-91.

5.34 The project is still relatively early in its life but has achieved success with residential schemes in progress and a studio/workshop scheme started with assistance through Urban Development Corporation expenditure and City Grant. In addition, improved fish handling facilities and tourist visitor facilities have helped economic development in the area.

Features

Area assessment: the environmental programme has been based on a comprehensive property, economic and environmental appraisal of the area as part of the preparation of the Urban Development Corporation area strategy.

Promotion and consultation: there has been extensive consultation with the local fishing industry and with local businesses and occupiers. The comprehensive approach to the area has been promoted both to indigenous businesses and to potential developers.

Development: potential development opportunities have been identified and promoted by the Urban Development Corporation, and subsequently supported with grant assistance.

Highways and infrastructure: rationalisation and improvement of quayside areas has provided practical benefits for fishing and tourism. Improved parking, street lighting and walkways have also been provided.

Property rehabilitation: grants have been provided for improvements to prominent buildings such as the local light houses which are still in use, or have been converted.

Amenity improvements: a wide range of small scale incremental environmental schemes have been undertaken such as repair to the quayside stairs, erection of a bronze dolphin (mooring post), planting and other small works.

Policy linkage: there has been a clear link between physical planning and economic development policies. This is particularly the case with the local fishing industry, but also more generally, for example in the support of studio/workshop development.

Grant assistance: part of the environmental improvement programme has involved direct grant assistance for the improvement of buildings as part of the development packages.

Funding mixture: in addition to grant assistance through environmental works, City Grant has been used to support individual development projects.

Casework Study 14

Nottingham and Beeston Canal, Nottingham

Urban Programme
Canal corridor area renewal to support and commercial use

Time: 1981-90
Expenditure: £0.23 million

Features

- Area assessment
- Development
- Partnership

- Promotion and consultation
- Amenity improvement
- Funding mixture

5.35 The Nottingham and Beeston Canal project was originally conceived by Nottingham City Council as an environmental and recreation strategy for a redundant canal. This was subsequently developed with British Waterways Board into an environmental strategy which provided the framework for attracting employment, residential and commercial development to the area. The elements of the strategy include marina, retail, hotel, residential and office developments together with a new Court House using the canal as a framework. Project implementation began in 1981 through Urban Programme funding, following earlier planning strategy assessments.

5.36 The Nottingham Beeston Canal scheme has been evolutionary. Before 1981 the recreational strategy sought modest improvements along the canalside. The succeeding strategy working with major landowners, British Waterways Board and British Rail, has successfully brought forward a rolling programme of residential, retail, commercial and leisure development within an integrated strategy which has enabled development to assist and complement canal improvements.

Features

Area assessment: the project was the subject of an assessment of the canal corridor as a whole for leisure use, and subsequent development of this to embrace commercial uses.

Promotion and consultation: this has been achieved working with the major landowners, British Waterways Board and British Rail.

Development: the area programme has allowed comprehensive solutions to be achieved for access and canalside improvements linked to development opportunities.

Amenity improvement: the environmental improvement of the canal corridor has been very successful in raising the general amenity of the area for leisure and commercial development.

Partnership: because of the concentration of land ownership with two statutory undertakers, an effective partnership has been required with the planning authority to co-ordinate development.

Fund mixture: Urban Development Grant and City Grant have been used to support development along the canal side.

Casework Study 15

Castlefield, Manchester

Urban Development Corporation		Time:	1989
Comprehensive commercial residential		Expenditure:	£2.5 million
inner area development			

Features

- Area assessment
- Highways
- Infrastructure
- Promotion
- Amenity improvements
- Development
- Grant assistance

5.37 Castlefield is one of the project areas of the Central Manchester Development Corporation. It is an area dominated by warehouses and canals, and containing low value industrial uses. The area was effectively closed to public access. A comprehensive environmental programme is being undertaken to open up the area and attract residential and commercial development. The programme has included floodlighting, building cleaning and canal restoration since 1989, and is continuing. Clearance of sites has been undertaken to improve the outlook of developments and release land for schemes. In the area, the Museum of Science and Industry, in a former railway terminus, has been supported through external environmental works.

5.38 The Castlefield scheme is still in the early stages of its life, but has achieved success. Reference has already been made to the Whitworth Street area improvements where grant assistance and the early lead from development have been fundamental in encouraging further residential schemes. In the Castlefield area the canalside improvements linked to development schemes at Castle Quay and Castlefield Basin have supported two office schemes (45,000ft^2) together with residential development (38 flats).

Features

Areas assessment: the Castlefield area was the subject of comprehensive property, economic and environmental assessment before the environmental improvement programme was initiated.

Promotion: the development sites and the area as a whole have been marketed extensively to developers.

Development: sites have been acquired and cleared by the Urban Development Corporation and either sold on for development or landscaped in association with other development sites.

Highways and infrastructure: the canal infrastructure has been rehabilitated to make areas safe for development and to provide an environmental framework for the area.

Amenity improvements: a range of improvements, particularly associated with canalside walkways have been used to link development sites and provide an environmental envelope for the area.

Grant assistance: some of the environmental improvements have involved cleaning of buildings' external elevations in association with rehabilitation projects in essentially grant assistance towards development costs.

Grant mixing: the development schemes have attracted additional assistance through City Grant.

Review of area programme case studies

5.39 The concluding element of this section reviews the overall findings of the area programme case studies and seeks to draw out some of the key messages in terms of:

- **A. CHARACTERISTICS**: (i) the evidence of the broad influence of the area programme approach,
  (ii) use,
  (iii) scale and
  (iv) differing urban policy programmes

- **B. FEATURES**: the role of the individual features identified.

A. Characteristics

i. The area programme approach

5.40 The case for area programme designation is that comprehensive focused action provides the potential to address problems at the area level, and to achieve economies of scale, project synergy and cumulative impact.

5.41 The case studies have demonstrated the success of the approach. EIP's have contributed to this success. The impact of EIP's however has been dependent on the effective application of an area based approach and the characteristics described below.

5.42 The case studies with the weaker economic impact tended to be those projects which moved away from the strengths of the area programme approach.

5.43 **Comprehensive project range:** case studies which provided for a range of integrated projects, for example development and highways as well as amenity works tended to provide for greater EIP impact (Closegate, Newcastle; New Ferry, Wirral). Case studies with one or only a few individual projects, particularly of a more diffuse nature, such as amenity improvement, tended to lack the interest, diversity and synergy of a multi-project programme (Blackbrook Valley, Greater Manchester Museum of Science and Industry).

5.44 **Area objectives:** clearly defined areas where function, identity and integrity can be supported provide a clear focus for an area approach to greatest effect (Whitworth Street, Manchester). Where areas were not effectively defined there appears to be a loss of focus, for example where boundaries are re-drawn this suggests a lack initial clarity in objectives (Ouseburn, Newcastle).

5.45 **Programming:** Effective programming and integration of projects are required based on a clear assessment of requirements and objectives for the area (North Shields and Fish Quay, Tyneside). Some of the programmes have not been established for areas until some years after inception. Without an overall framework the area programme has suffered from a lack of overall direction and momentum in the interim (Hyson Green, Nottingham; Ouseburn, Newcastle). Similarly, successive revisions to programming have not assisted in providing the clarity of objectives and momentum that a programme should provide (Lace Market, Nottingham).

5.46 Timescale: programme timescales can influence the momentum and direction of projects, although these need to be seen in the context of the scale and condition of an area and available budgets; foreshortened programme timescales reflect effective programming (Closegate, Newcastle). It is a feature of those programmes with a weaker focus or with less emphasis on programming that their timescales have been extended -in some cases over 10 years, or longer if action through other regimes is included. Others which have been comprehensive, focused and ordered in their programming have completed their objectives more quickly (New Ferry, Wirral, North Shields).

ii. Area Uses

5.47 The programmes selected have, with three exceptions, been focused on single uses as a characteristic which defines an area. The different uses have had an influence on the impact of EIPs.

> **Retail:** retailing has demonstrated a strong response to EIP programmes where these have been effectively implemented (New Ferry, Wirral). Important features have been both improvements to the physical arrangement of areas, through pedestrianisation and development, and also improvements to visual amenity. Property improvement grants are a feature which supported by improvements to infrastructure and highways have attracted private sector investment. Retail activity is sensitive to the quality of its environment. Retail environments are important in seeking to attract and retain shoppers in competition with other centres.

> **Commercial:** the City Centre projects have also responded to a mixture of improvement of the physical arrangement and visual amenity. Economic regeneration however has appeared less dynamic and required a longer period to take effect over a wider area (Lace Market, Nottingham). The economic limitations even for areas very close to the central area suggests that regeneration is an incremental process and major development which may overreach the strengths of the area (Mathew Street, Liverpool) without continuing EIP support. The inner area projects appear to place more emphasis on accessibility and service rather than visual amenity (New Basford, Ouseburn,Stoney Lane). This in part reflects the more general industrial, rather than office related uses in these locations.

> **Residential:** the limited evidence is that for the residential area based programme which had a strong emphasis on visual amenity there was a relatively weaker development response to EIPs. The more significant impacts were achieved through grant subsidy and the demonstration effects of completed projects (Whitworth Street, Manchester). Residential environments appear relatively self-contained, particularly in City Centres. Developers appear to focus on the internal environment they are seeking to create, rather than the more general area wide perceptions.

> **Leisure:** the hotel and leisure case studies suggest that such developments are essentially free standing from their surrounding environment. In the

case of hotel projects, road communications and, where in central areas, links to the City Centre are important as business custom is the principal market. The larger leisure schemes are an attraction in their own right, and are also freestanding. (Greater Manchester Museum of Science and Industry; Closegate, Newcastle). However, the case studies suggest that leisure uses, including public open space, can assist in providing an enhanced environment and a focus for residential (Watery Lane, Walsall) and commercial (Closegate, Newcastle) development where there are strong physical links with the environmental improvements.

Mixed use: the success of mixed use programmes emphasises the point that use may be a convenient characteristic for defining the boundaries of an area programme, but wider consideration needs to be give to the characteristics of integrity of an area and the potential benefits of integrated and complementary uses. The integration of commercial, tourism and residential uses has worked well in a location which has a strong overall identity (North Shields, Tyneside). In other cases the integration of leisure and public open space and commercial development has combined effectively to provide a first class environment (Nottingham and Beeston Canal).

iii. Scale

5.48 The scale of the area programmes has ranged from under six acres (Stoney Lane, Rainhill) to in excess of seventy acres (Lace Market, Nottingham). There is no evidence of a fixed relationship between scale and success. The key factor is the scale of resources and commitment relative to the area and its needs. Some projects with extended areas have been able to mount sustained programmes to meet the size and nature of the problem (Lace Market, Nottingham). Others have adopted small focused project areas appropriate to the resources available (Mathew Street, Liverpool).

5.49 Where the scale of an area programme becomes an issue is when the programme is under-resourced. There then appears a tendency to adopt a more attenuated, incremental approach with less momentum (Ouseburn, Newcastle).

iv. Urban policy programmes

5.50 The features of the different policy programmes are reflected in the individual projects.

5.51 **Urban programme:** programmes have become increasingly focused in approach with the establishment of area programmes and planning. At the same time there has been a movement towards concentration of resources on either larger projects or smaller target areas rather than a spread of resources on a wide range of small scale incremental projects. This has increased the success of projects, but there still remain practical problems of achieving an assured continuity of funding for longer running area projects, with only limited commitment to projects extending beyond the immediate annual budget.

5.52 Some of the features of Urban Programme do not always assist area development:

- Budgets are approved annually with only limited commitment to funding beyond the current budget year. This can lead to uncertainty and potential loss of momentum (New Ferry, Wirral).

- Concentration on a diversity of small scale projects to allow flexibility for budget programming may in the past have led to less effective action (Ouseburn, Newcastle). This, however, is now being corrected with emphasis on co-ordinated and concentrated funding for larger projects (Lace Market, Nottingham).

5.53 **Urban Development Corporations:** commitment to sustained funding over a Corporation's lifetime, integrated with physical planning and development programming provides an effective approach to area development, as evidenced in the case studies (North Shields and Fish Quay, Tyneside).

5.54 **Derelict Land Grant:** larger projects have benefited from a continuing commitment for funding supported by Derelict Land Programmes. The effective integration of land reclamation with wider development and economic planning policies is dependent on individual planning authorities. In some cases effective linkage at the area level may be more difficult to achieve, for example, where Local Authorities do not exercise Development Control, as in Enterprise Zones (Blackbrook Valley, Dudley).

B. Features

5.55 **Area assessment:** the foundation for effective EIP area programming is a clear assessment of economic and environmental potential and constraints, together with a comprehensive planned programme in response to the specific problems of the area and with defined objectives. This was provided at the outset as the basis for the most successful programmes (New Ferry, Wirral; Closegate, Newcastle).

5.56 For some of the smaller projects the lack of this approach was less important (Stoney Lane, Rainhill). In the larger schemes the lack of a comprehensive view at the outset appears to have hindered progress both in effectively co-ordinating action, and promoting area improvements to developers and occupiers (Hyson Green, Nottingham).

5.57 **Promotion and consultation: for area-based EIPs:** these have been a feature of successful projects. Consultation has tended to be a feature of Urban Programme schemes working with existing occupiers and businesses (New Ferry, Wirral; New Basford, Nottingham). This has also been used as an opportunity to promote the area.

5.58 Promotion has also been an important feature of Urban Development Corporation projects where the emphasis and expertise in corporate promotion has effectively marketed locations to developers (Closegate, Newcastle; North Shields, Tyneside).

5.59 Promotion and consultation has been seen to be less in evidence in the Derelict Land Grant projects, but reflects the fact that both case studies were essentially focused on the provision of amenity space rather than direct development investment.

5.60 **Development:** linkage of area programme EIPs to specific development opportunities has been important in facilitating development investment. This has usually required the public agency concerned to acquire and assemble sites, undertake clearance and servicing and then promote these opportunities (Mathew Street, Liverpool; New Basford, Nottingham). In other cases there has been close involvement with developers committed to schemes (Whitworth Street, Manchester).

5.61 Where the property market has been too weak to attract private sector development investment, public agencies have assumed the development role to assist occupiers (Lace Market, Nottingham; Ouseburn, Newcastle).

5.62 **Highways and infrastructure:** provision has been an important feature in EIP area improvement programmes. This has given enhanced accessibility, removed the constraints of pedestrian-vehicle conflict in areas where pedestrianisation has been possible (New Ferry, Wirral; Lace Market, Nottingham), and improved parking facilities in inner areas. Highways and infrastructure provision have improved locations' communications and also provided a physical framework for development and further environmental improvement.

5.63 **Property rehabilitation:** has been a key feature in retaining the character and established business in inner areas (Whitworth Street, Manchester; Lace Market, Nottingham). This has for the most part involved building repair grants to owners and occupiers for external works. Internal repair and reorganisation of buildings have been left to the initiative of owners and occupiers, sometimes with the assistance of City Grant. Rehabilitation of sites, as well as buildings, has also contributed to the environment for investment. Projects whose principal emphasis was amenity, particularly in industrial areas, appear to have had modest impact in terms of attracting new development investment, at least in the short term.

5.64 **Amenity Improvements:** improvements to visual amenity of the area have been a common feature of almost all programmes. This has been most effective where it has been in conjunction with other features, for example, highways and infrastructure (New Ferry, Wirral) or development (Closegate, Newcastle). To date, such projects appear less effective in the attraction of development investment where they have stood alone (Blackbrook Valley, Dudley; Greater Manchester Museum of Science and Technology).

5.65 **Policy linkage:** the effectiveness of EIPs has benefited from being reinforced by complementary area policies. Town Schemes have allowed access to supporting grant funding from English Heritage (Mathew Street, Liverpool). Projects in Urban Development Corporation areas have benefited from the integration of planning and development promotion and corporate marketing. In Nottingham, Council Capital Programme expenditure in support of the textile industry has allowed direct development (Lace Market, Nottingham).

5.66 **Partnership:** only in one recent case has a formal partnership between the public and private sector been established for development investment (Lace Market, Nottingham). It is too early to establish whether this arrangement will secure additional development investment, but this approach has now been duplicated by other Inner Area Authorities.

5.67 **Grant assistance:** EIP programmes have provided direct grant assistance for development as a subsidy to land and construction costs. Examples include clearance and sale of sites (New Basford, Nottingham), grant subsidies for repairs (Ouseburn, Newcastle), and in some cases meeting the extra costs of external block repair (New Ferry, Wirral).

5.68 **Programming and timescale:** many of the area programmes are still in their early stages, particularly in the case of Urban Development Corporations. The contrast between long running and shorter programmes is most apparent in Urban Programme projects. Although there are different and difficult local circumstances, it is apparent in some cases (Hyson Green, Nottingham) a lack of initial comprehensive area assessment and planning has meant that the initial programme years were to an extent unstructured and unfocused, contributing to a lack of momentum. This contrasts with the benefits of a clear programmed approach (New Ferry, Wirral) which demonstrated an effective programme application over a short timescale.

5.69 **Funding Mixture:** funding diversity and combination of sources have helped expand the range of resources and their application. These have included private sector sources, City Grant and Urban Development Grant (Whitworth Street, Manchester) and public sector sources, English Heritage, ERDF and Council Capital budgets (Lace Market, Nottingham).

6 Case studies: site projects

Site projects

6.1 This section examines a selection of site specific Environmental Improvement Projects, their impacts and key features. This provides a basis for examining the overall findings of the impacts of EIPs on urban regeneration in Section 7. In each case we have provided a project summary and outlined the important EIP features.

6.2 Site projects are EIPs undertaken in respect of individual sites to attract private investment, rather than as part of an area programme, although in some cases they may have a general relationship with other projects in the surrounding area.

6.3 **Project objectives:** the immediate objectives are defined in terms of output measures; development, reclamation and intended after use. The case studies selected had all achieved their project objectives, or were progressing to their end stage.

6.4 The case studies are divided between the following categories:

- **Commercial:** Building Rehabilitation

   Smaller Site Development (under 10 acres)

   Larger Site Development (over 10 acres)

- **Residential:** Smaller Site Development (under 10 acres)

   Larger Site Development (over 10 acres)

Commercial projects: building rehabilitation

Casework Study 1

Former Gerard Gamble Building, Nottingham

Urban Programme
Refurbishment of city centre commercial
building for textile workshops

Time: 1980, 1990-
Expenditure: £1.11 million
(including other grant sources)

Features

- Project Assessment
- Amenity Improvement
- Development
- Policy Linkage
- Property Rehabilitation

6.5   The former Gerard Gamble Building is a four storey Victorian commercial building which occupies a gateway position at the southern approach to Nottingham City Centre. Formerly used for textile production, the building was occupied by catering equipment manufacturers for showroom and storage uses. A modest grant was given initially towards repairs through Urban Programme. The occupiers subsequently vacated the building, which became the subject of speculation as to alternative uses including casino and club, or offices through redevelopment or refurbishment. During this time, the building deteriorated. The City Council acquired the building and is refurbishing the premises for textile workshops in support of its policy to retain indigenous industry in the area.

6.6   The refurbishment of the Gerard Gamble building is still in progress and therefore final assessment is premature. An earlier attempt to support the continued maintenance of the building through a modest grant for repair did not secure the longer term future of the building. It underlines the difficulties of safeguarding buildings whose commercial future is marginal, the limits to modest repair work where buildings require rehabilitation and renewal, and the importance of a clear property market assessment to identify definitive potential after use to which environmental works can be linked.

Features

Project assessment: the initial repair grant was essentially to safeguard the building. However, without reference to the intended final use this was speculative and whilst desirable for amenity objectives did not demonstrate clear economic aims. The subsequent development by the Council required a full project assessment.

Development: the City Council has had to undertake the role of developer because the project is not commercially viable, although it is anticipated that there is a reasonable demand from occupiers from the textile industry. The principal objective is to support investment in the textile industry rather than the attraction of private sector investment in property.

Property rehabilitation: the project will save a prominent building which forms part of the historic industrial core of the City.

Amenity improvement: the building occupies a prominent gateway site to the south of the City Centre. The project therefore offers the wider benefits of enhancing the immediate environs.

Policy linkage: the Council's economic policy to support the indigenous textile industry thorough provision of accommodation underwrote environmental policies to save and convert the building.

Grant assistance: the development has been funded entirely through grant sources without private sector investment in the scheme.

Funding Mixture: the City Council applied Capital Programme and European Regional Development Grant Finance as well as Urban Programme.

Figure 6.1 Case studies: site project features

Project	Project assessment	Promotion & consultation	Development	Highways & infrastructure	Property rehabilitation	Amenity improvement	Policy linkage	Partnership	Grant assistance	Other
Building rehabilitation										
Gerard Gamble Building, Nottingham	●		●		●	●	●			Funding mixture
Daisyfield Mill, Blackburn	●	●	●	●		●	●		●	Funding mixture
South Sefton BC, Bootle	●	●	●		●	●		●	●	Funding mixture
Commercial: smaller sites										
Qualcast Site, Wolverhampton	●	●	●			●				
Bentley Site, Walsall	●		●				●	●	●	Funding mixture
Commercial: larger sites										
Newhallhey, Rawtenstall	●		●	●		●	●		●	Funding mixture
GEC Site, Clayton-le-Moors Westwood Power Station, Wigan	●		●	●		●	●		●	
Residential: smaller sites										
Black Lake, West Bromwich	●	●	●			●				
Blakeley Hall, West Bromwich	●	●	●			●			●	
Chad Road, Bamford, Dudley	●	●	●			●			●	
Residential: larger sites										
Towneley Brickworks, Burnley	●		●			●		●	●	Funding mixture
Moseley Common, Wigan	●		●			●		●	●	
St Peters Marina, Newcastle	●	●	●	●		●		●	●	
St Peters Riverside, Sunderland	●	●	●	●		●			●	

Casework study 2

Daisyfield Mill, Blackburn

Derelict Land Grant
Inner area mill conversion

Time: 1986-91
Expenditure: £0.05 million
(including other grant sources)

Features

- Project assessment
- Infrastructure
- Policy linkage
- Promotion and consultation
- Property rehabilitation
- Grant assistance
- Development
- Amenity improvement
- Funding mixture

6.7   Daisyfield Mill, Blackburn, is located in an inner industrial area. The building was acquired by Lancashire Enterprises, Lancashire County Council's economic development agency, working with the Local Authority and former building owners, Graham and Brown. Using Derelict Land Grant and ERDF funding the building has been converted to workshops and offices together with clearance and landscaping of external areas and canalside improvements. The workshop/office complex is managed by Lancashire Enterprises. The mill lies in the Leeds-Liverpool canal corridor which is the focus of an integrated programme of economic and environmental projects.

6.8   Daisyfield Mill has so far had mixed success. The restoration of the mill building and the improvement of the adjoining canalside area have made an impressive visual contribution and removed dereliction along the canalside. The local economy, however, remains relatively depressed, and further development has not been attracted to the area. In addition, there is temporary oversupply of small workshop/office units and lettings in the mill have been slow, with competing projects nearby. The longer term benefits of the scheme are likely to be established, if slowly.

Features

Project assessment: the development of the mill was the subject of a property market and feasibility appraisal to identify market potential and accommodation demand.

Promotion and consultation: there was active involvement of the mill owners who sold the property to the County Council ensuring that the building continued in beneficial use.

Development: the clearance and landscaping works funded by Derelict Land Grant were an integral element of the scheme and linked to the development objectives of the project as a whole.

Infrastructure: in this case there were limited repairs to the canal wall.

Property rehabilitation: the scheme has secured the refurbishment of a major building which otherwise would probably have deteriorated or been cleared in common with other mills in the area.

Amenity improvement: the mill is a prominent and attractive building (Grade II listed) and also lies within canal corridor which is an important local amenity.

Policy linkage: the project links with wider economic and environmental policy objectives. The economic policy objectives include business development and training through the involvement of Lancashire Enterprises. The project is also part of the strategic economic and environmental programme for the Leeds-Liverpool Canal Corridor which focuses EC support for upgrading the canal area through environmental improvement and economic development.

Grant assistance: Derelict Land Grant helped to underwrite the viability of the development.

Funding mixture: the project has drawn on a range of grant sources in addition to DLG, including Urban Programme, ERDF and Training Agency support.

Casework study 3

South Sefton Business Centre, Bootle, Merseyside

Urban Programme	Time:	1989-91
Conversion of derelict industrial building into a Business Centre	Expenditure:	£0.45 million

Features

- Project assessment
- Property rehabilitation
- Policy linkage
- Promotion and consultation
- Amenity improvement
- Funding mixture
- Development
- Policy linkage

6.9   South Sefton Business Centre was created as part of the comprehensive redevelopment of a former administrative building on an inner area industrial estate, linked to clearance and reclamation of the remaining site for a subsequent phase of small industrial unit development. The site and building were formerly derelict and occupied by alcohol and drug abusers, which led to local businesses approaching the Council to take action. The Local Authority's Enterprise Agency is represented in the Business Centre and provides business advice and supporting services for the area. Negotiations are being progressed with private sector partners for the development of the small industrial units.

6.10 The South Sefton Business Centre has been a highly successful project to date. Since completion in Spring 1991, the scheme has been fully let providing accommodation for small businesses, and support and advice to the wider business community. If current negotiations are successful the second phase of industrial units will attract private sector funding. The wider objectives of the scheme, to assist in the regeneration of the surrounding area generally, will take longer to achieve. Businesses in the area have limited resources to commit to new investment to improve their premises, even with grant assistance. Earlier general environmental works to the area including planting and off-street parking areas have not proved successful because of vandalism and crime in the area. Future environmental improvements will need to be strongly linked to development and existing business premises.

Features

Project assessment: the Business Centre was the subject of a full property market appraisal and feasibility study which identified potential serviced office demand. The rapid occupancy of the accommodation has fully justified this.

Promotion and consultation: the Council's selection of the site for the Business Centre followed local business concerns as to its dereliction and use by drug users. The Business Centre provides services and advice across the South Sefton area and promotes the location to potential business. In the immediate area the Centre has been a focus for environmental improvements and there has been continuing promotion and dialogue with local firms to encourage take up of grant assistance for improvements to firms' premises.

Development: the environmental works have been directly linked to development, both in the initial phase with the Council developing the Business Centre, and with the promotion of the second phase to be undertaken by the private sector.

Amenity improvement: the scheme is a significant improvement of the local environment, both removing dereliction and providing a high quality redevelopment scheme as a focus for area wide improvement.

Policy linkage: the scheme forms part of the Council's economic and development strategy for the Maritime Area - supporting new and existing businesses with advice and accommodation, and seeking to provide an enhanced environment.

Funding mixture: the Council has drawn on Derelict Land Grant and Merseyside Development Corporation assistance in addition to Urban Programme.

Casework study 4

Qualcast Site, Wolverhampton

Derelict Land Grant   Time: 1983-90
Industrial site reclamation   Expenditure: £0.41 million

Features

- Project assessment
- Promotion and consultation
- Development
- Amenity improvement

6.11   The Qualcast site was a former foundry and occupies a prominent location on the main road between Wolverhampton and the M6 motorway. The site was cleared, landscaped and a new access road and services provided for new industrial development, using Derelict Land Grant and ERDF support. West Midlands County Council and Wolverhampton MBC, who completed the project, identified a shortage of smaller serviced sites for industrial development in the area. This was not being met by the private sector because low development values would not support commercial development.

6.12   The scheme has been successful with over half of the site (1.7 ha) taken by a local firm requiring new premises and a higher quality environment. The firm would otherwise have relocated outside the area. The balance of the site (0.5 ha) is the subject of negotiations with another local company whose existing premises are affected by road proposals. In addition redevelopment of the site will include environmental works to the perimeters and canal frontage.

Features

Project assessment: the scheme was the subject of site supply and demand assessment by the Borough Council before the project was executed.

Promotion and consultation: consultations were held with adjoining land owners and occupiers, and Black Country Development Corporation over the options for servicing additional land. The Council has successfully promoted the site to potential occupiers.

Development: the project's objective to attract private sector development has been successfully achieved. Comprehensive development of the site would have been unlikely without the Council's initiative.

Amenity improvement: the removal of former dereliction, and the opportunity taken to secure environmental works to the site boundaries have assisted in modest improvement to the local amenity.

Casework study 5

Bentley Site, Walsall

Derelict Land Grant
Hotel site reclamation

Time: 1983-89
Expenditure: £0.55 million

Features

- Project assessment
- Partnership

- Development
- Grant assistance

- Policy linkage
- Funding mixture

6.13 The Bentley site is situated at Junction 10 of the M6 motorway. The land was derelict and contained mine workings and a shaft which needed to be capped before development. Walsall MBC identified the requirement for a hotel in the area as part of the economic development of the Borough, and the development potential offered by the site. This was supported by DoE, DTI and the Heart of England Tourist Board. The Tourist Board marketed the site to hotel operators, and attracted a developer and operator. A combination of Derelict Land Grant and Urban Development Grant was used to reclaim the site and support the hotel development. In addition, environmental works were undertaken at the site entrance supported by Urban Programme funding.

6.14 The scheme has attracted a national hotel developer and operator who had previously only developed in greenfield locations. The company would not have assembled the package necessary to reclaim the site and undertake the project itself. The hotel is an addition to the services in the local economy.

Features

Project assessment: the Council's working with the local Tourism Board identified a lack of hotel provision in the area and successfully identified a budget hotel developer.

Development: without site acquisition and reclamation the development would not have taken place. The hotel operators had neither the interest nor the knowledge to assemble the appropriate grant package and execute the technical work to allow redevelopment.

Policy linkage: the hotel development formed part of the Council's wider economic strategy to promote supporting services and employment in the area.

Partnership: the Council worked closely with the hotel developer in planning and executing land reclamation and environmental works to ensure that the site was reclaimed and landscaped to the required specification.

Funding mixture: the project included additional funding from City Grant and Urban Programme.

Casework Study 6

Newhallhey Mill, Rawtenstall

Derelict Land Grant
Site reclamation linked to mill
and railway restoration

Time :   1985-90
Expenditure: £0.6 million
(net after capital receipts)

Features

- Project assessment
- Policy linkage
- Development
- Grant assistance
- Highways and Infrastructure
- Funding Mixture

6.15 Newhallhey Mill, Rawtenstall is a prominent building situated beside the Haslingden-Edenfield by-pass (A65T) which links the M66/M62 motorways and the Manchester conurbation with the M65 motorway to the north. The mill was vacant and in decay with the balance of the site unstable because of earlier deposits of fill. Lancashire Enterprises Limited, the County Council's Economic Development Agency, acquired the property. The mill was converted to provide managed workspace, with out buildings converted for use by the Groundwork Trust as offices, interpretation centre and hostel. The balance of the site (11 acres) was reclaimed, with a new access from the by-pass, access road and services. The site was sold for business, hotel and retail development. The project was funded by Derelict Land Grant and ERDF. The scheme complements projects in the immediate area including redevelopment of an adjoining former coal depot for retail and office use, the re-opening of the East Lancashire Railway with a new station adjoining the site, and environmental improvements to the River Irwell and buildings nearby.

6.16 The reclamation and environmental works at the Newhallhey Mill site have transformed a derelict industrial site into an attractive development location for higher quality business and leisure uses at a focal point on the main road approach to Rawtenstall. Private sector development in this location will also reinforce other initiatives in the environs. The take-up of accommodation in the restored mill has been slow, with about a quarter of the floorspace let, but the improving area and general economic prospects should increase lettings.

Features

Project assessment: the initial catalyst for site reclamation arose from the proposals for purchase and restoration of the mill using ERDF funding. There was not a market assessment for the reclaimed site beyond before and after use valuation. However, the site was well located beside the bypass and attracted developer interest when it was marketed.

Development: the reclamation and servicing were undertaken to support development. Without these being completed and because of access and highways uncertainties in addition, it is unlikely that the site could have been promoted effectively to developers.

Highways and infrastructure: one way access directly from the new bypass was included in the scheme, and there are now proposals for improvement to a full two way junction. It is uncertain whether without Local Authority promotion a private sector developer could have secured access from the by-pass, or would have been prepared to initiate discussions for this.

Policy linkage: the reclamation scheme is closely linked with a range of wider policies. The rehabilitation of the mill has been supported by building conservation and environmental polices, as well as economic development in the provision of serviced business space. In addition, the re-opening of the East Lancashire Railway line adjoining the site will provide enhanced tourism and commuter links. More generally, the reclamation of the site complements a programme of environmental projects improving the southern approach to the town.

Grant assistance: the works undertaken have assisted in underwriting the future development viability of the reclaimed site.

Funding mixture: funding has also been drawn from ERDF sources for the mill building conversion, and from Groundwork Trust for environmental and interpretative centre projects.

Casework study 7

GEC Site, Clayton-le-Moors

| Derelict Land Grant | Time: | 1984-6 |
| Industrial site reclamation and servicing | Expenditure: | £0.7 million |

Features

- Project assessment
- Amenity improvement
- Development
- Grant assistance
- Highways and infrastructure
- Funding mixture

6.17 The GEC site forms part of an engineering complex located within two minutes drive of the M65 motorway. The land was released from operational requirements but contained foundations and bases of former buildings together with waste residues. The land was granted Enterprise Zone (EZ) status as part of the West Lancashire Enterprise Zone. Despite the attraction of excellent road communications and EZ benefits, the site failed to attract private sector interest because of the scale of comprehensive clearance and servicing required. Lancashire County Council acquired the site and undertook clearance, landscaping and servicing using Derelict Land Grant. On completion the site was sold to developers who undertook a series of design and build, and speculative projects.

6.18 Development on the GEC site has now been completed with all the sites in the Enterprise Zone occupied and accommodation totalling 130,500 ft^2. The location and communications, and the quality of the reclamation and environment have attracted high specification business space development, as well as industrial and commercial uses. The site services and access have also supported development on adjoining sites.

Features

Project assessment: an initial assessment of the demand and supply of industrial land was undertaken to establish the potential for development prior to EZ designation. A further assessment was made after the site had failed to secure developer interest following EZ designation. This confirmed the potential for development and the constraints of site conditions. The proposed works provided for a comprehensive approach to removing the site constraints.

Development: the site reclamation, landscaping and servicing were undertaken as a basis for development.

Highways and infrastructure: site access and services were required before developer interest could be secured.

Amenity improvement: the quality of the landscaping within the scheme has created an enhanced environment which has encouraged high quality development, taking advantage of the excellent road communications.

Grant assistance: the procurement of site access and services has provided a subsidy to development. This has been partially offset through the proceeds of site sale, reducing net reclamation costs to under £25,000 per acre. In theory development could have been undertaken without direct public sector action, using City Grant subsidy. In practice developers were not prepared to undertake the investment risk of reclaiming and servicing such a large site.

Funding mixture: the project is linked with the EZ designation which, although not a grant regime, provides subsidy to developers and occupiers through capital allowances and business rate exemptions.

Casework study 8

Westwood Power Station, Wigan

Derelict Land Grant
Industrial land renewal and development

Time: 1987
Expenditure: £0.09 million
(£1.2 million proposed)

Features

- Project assessment
- Development
- Highways and infrastructure
- Amenity improvement
- Grant assistance

6.19 Westwood Power Station is located a quarter of a mile from Wigan town centre and adjoins the Wigan Flashes Geological Park which is the subject of progressive reclamation using Derelict Land Grant and Countryside Commission funding. The power station site totals some 90 acres and was occupied by an operational power station until 1986. The site was acquired by Wigan MBC using Derelict Land Grant for comprehensive clearance and redevelopment, and is to be served by the proposed M6-M61 motorway link. The site was identified by Girobank who were seeking a location for a new processing centre. The bank subsequently acquired part of the site (16 acres) which was cleared and serviced by Wigan MBC using Derelict Land Grant. The initial phase of the Girobank development totals 86,000ft^2 and will employ 650 persons when fully operational. The balance of the power station site is the subject of discussion with potential private sector development partners for reclamation, servicing and redevelopment.

6.20 The reclamation of the Westwood Power Station site has successfully attracted Girobank. This has provided an initial impetus to the reclamation and development of the balance of the site in partnership with the private sector. Redevelopment here complements the progressive reclamation of the Wigan Flashes nearby and the general improvement of the canal corridor. Development of direct links with the motorway network will provide the necessary communications to support further development on the site.

Features

Project assessment: Wigan MBC undertook a review of the site in the context of strategic site supply and demand and identified the location as offering development potential. The assessment included environmental considerations and the proximity of the site both to the town centre and to the surrounding countryside.

Development: the programme of land reclamation and servicing is directly linked to the promotion of development on the site. Girobank would not have considered the location unless clearance, site access and services had been committed by the Council.

Highways and infrastructure: the scheme provides new access and services to the site and is programmed to connect with the proposed M6-M61 motorway link.

Amenity improvement: the scheme complements the programme of restoration and management of Wigan Flashes Geological Park and canal corridor improvement as an attractive environmental context for development.

Grant assistance: the clearance of the power station together with services and access works has assisted in underwriting the development viability of the project.

Casework study 9

Black Lake, West Bromwich

Derelict Land Grant
Reclamation of railway sidings for
residential development

Time: 1987-9
Expenditure: £0.45 million

Features

- Project assessment
- Amenity improvement
- Promotion
- Funding mixture
- Development

6.21   The site (7.7 acres) lies between Wednesbury and West Bromwich, surrounded by a mixed commercial and residential environment. A feature of the site is the Ridgrove Branch Canal which forms one boundary with the towpath identified as a potential walkway project by the Local Authority. The land was made ground for former railway sidings and also included two mineshafts and tanks from a former petrol station. Additional site constraints included the need for a drainage easement over adjoining Council owned land, and a high voltage electricity cable which crossed the site with a pylon situated within the site boundary.

6.22   British Rail as land owners were unsuccessful in marketing the site for residential development. Sandwell MBC acquired and reclaimed the site using Derelict Land Grant. The site was subsequently sold for residential development with land receipts exceeding total costs. In addition canal side improvements were undertaken to provide a walkway and public open space. The project won a Royal Town Planning Institute commendation.

6.23   The project has been very successful. An unpromising site was identified as having development potential, and reclaimed and sold for approaching £0.9 million, compared with the cost of acquisition and subsequent reclamation of £0.45 million. An estimated £4.1 million private sector investment was attracted. The opportunity was taken to link this to canalside improvements, which although having a limited relationship with the housing, provide an environmental buffer and are an element in the longer term canalside improvement programme.

Features

Project assessment: a full assessment of ground conditions and servicing requirements was undertaken as a basis for reclamation for development. The Council also assessed the demand for residential land in this location including establishing initial interest, in principle, from developers.

Promotion: the site was marketed with a clear planning and development brief providing the policy framework, development considerations and design guidance. Information was also supplied on ground conditions and services. This approach provided for effective marketing and helped to remove the uncertainties which formerly deterred private sector investment.

Development: the site was reclaimed for the purposes of residential development, together with adjoining canal side improvements. Reclamation was a pre-requisite to attract developer interest. The reclamation has provided no net grant support to underwrite development viability, with sale proceeds exceeding costs. However, developers were not prepared to assume the initial risk of reclamation and servicing for the site.

Amenity improvement: the reclamation and redevelopment of the site provided wider amenity benefits in providing a clear boundary to established residential areas and complementing the canalside improvements. However, the residential development has been designed to provide clear separation from the public area beside the canal. There is a degree of mutual support between the public and private areas, but the estate layout has been arranged to create its own internal environment isolated from the unattractive environs, and managing to accommodate a high voltage pylon and cable which passes over the site.

Funding mixture: Urban Programme funding was used to undertake the canalside improvements in addition to Derelict Land Grant used for the main site.

Casework study 10

Blakeley Hall, West Bromwich

Derelict Land Grant		Time:	1985-8
Reclamation of derelict site for industrial development		Expenditure:	£0.08 million

Features

- Project assessment
- Development
- Amenity improvement
- Promotion

6.24 The site (0.71 acres) is a gap frontage to the Birmingham Road, formerly occupied by a petrol filling station. The surrounding residential environment is poor and affected by heavy traffic volumes. The site was offered for sale for residential development in a derelict condition by the owners, without success. Sandwell MBC acquired and reclaimed the site using Derelict Land Grant. The site was subsequently sold at a price in excess of grant costs, and residential development completed.

6.25 The Blakeley Hall Gardens scheme has successfully consolidated residential use in a location where the environment is very poor. The removal of the derelict petrol station has also enhanced the outlook of the surrounding dwellings. The site sale proceeds, £134,000, substantially exceeded the costs of acquisition and reclamation, £85,000. The private sector was previously unwilling to invest in the site when it was offered prior to reclamation.

Features

Project assessment: a full assessment of ground conditions was undertaken as a basis for reclamation for development. The Council also assessed the demand for residential land in this location including establishing initial interest, in principle, from developers.

Promotion: the site was marketed with a clear planning and development brief providing the policy framework, development considerations and design guidance. Information was also supplied on ground conditions and services. This approach provided for effective marketing and helped to remove the uncertainties which formerly deterred private sector investment.

Development: the site was reclaimed for the purposes of residential development . Without reclamation there would have been no interest from developers.

Amenity improvement: the reclamation and redevelopment of the site has been a benefit to the surrounding residential area in an unattractive environment. The inward focus of the estate layout has managed to create its own environment.

Casework study 11

Chad Road, Bamford

Derelict Land Grant
Reclamation of quarry for residential development

Time: 1985-9
Expenditure: Estimated £1.26 million

Features

- Project assessment
- Promotion
- Development
- Amenity Improvement

6.26   The site (9.6 acres) was a quarry and subsequently used for tipping of foundry tailings. The land adjoins an established residential area. The infill was unstable and contained toxic residues. The quarry was acquired by West Midlands CC, with reclamation subsequently completed by Dudley MBC. The project was financed through Derelict Land Grant. The site was sold for residential development and a successful scheme has now been completed.

6.27   The reclamation and redevelopment of the site has been very successful. An attractive high quality residential scheme has been undertaken, and a potentially dangerous quarry tip removed. The reclamation has been complex and costly, £1.26 million including acquisition. However, site sale proceeds significantly exceeded this, £2.6 million, and attracted substantial private sector development and investment.

Features

Project assessment: a full assessment of ground conditions was undertaken as a basis for reclamation for residential development. The potential market demand for residential development was also tested, in principle, with developers.

Promotion: the site was marketed with a clear planning and development brief providing the policy framework, development considerations and design guidance. Information was also supplied on ground conditions and services. This approach provided for effective marketing and helped to remove the uncertainties which formerly deterred private sector investment.

Development: the site was reclaimed for the purpose of residential development. Reclamation by the public sector was a pre-requisite for developer interest.

Amenity improvement: the removal of the quarry has contributed to public safety with the site adjoining a school and residential area. More generally the quarry was well screened so did not have a major impact on surrounding environments.

Residential schemes: larger sites

Casework study 12

Townley Brickworks, Burnley

Derelict Land Grant
Reclamation of former brickworks for
residential use and public open space

Time   1988-91
Expenditure: £0.32 million

Features

- Project assessment
- Partnership
- Development
- Funding mixture
- Amenity improvement

6.28 The site (14 acres) lies on the south side of Burnley in an elevated position overlooking open country and adjoining an established residential area. The owners of the brickworks, which were no longer operational, approached and agreed the sale of the land to the County Council for reclamation using Derelict Land Grant. The agreement provided that the owner would repurchase part of the reclaimed site at development value if residential planning permission was granted, with the balance (9 acres) retained by the County Council as public open space.

6.29 Reclamation involved clearance of extensive workings and capping mineshafts. The site owners negotiated an agreement with housebuilders for sale and development on completion of clearance works. The sale of part of the site by the County Council to the brickworks owners at £480,000 exceeded costs of reclamation and landscaping to the remaining public open space (£327,000). On completion the project is anticipated to have attracted private sector investment of £3.8 million.

6.30   The scheme successfully removed dereliction and promoted the development of housing and provision of public open space. Without the support of Derelict Land Grant the landowners would not have brought the site forward for development because of the costs and risk involved in reclamation, and the uncertainties of achieving planning permission for residential development.

Features

Project assessment: the potential demand for residential land was assessed by the land owners in advance of approaching the County Council and was reflected in the agreed price for the repurchase of land for sale on to a residential developer.

Development: the reclamation was directly linked to the provision of residential development. Without the County Council assuming the risk of the reclamation and supporting the case for residential planning permission on the site the land owners would not have progressed the scheme. The complexity of reclamation has required that planning and reclamation be integrated with the establishment of estate site layouts at the initial stage.

Amenity improvement: the removal of a prominent derelict site has had a beneficial impact on the environs. The provision of public open space has also provided an amenity for the area and an effective use for site areas which could not be reclaimed for development.

Partnership: the scheme was based on a partnership with the landowner with a legal agreement for reclamation and resale, conditional on residential planning permission.

Funding mixture: limited funding was also provided by the Countryside Commission for landscaping works associated with the public open space.

Casework Study 13

Moseley Common, Wigan

Derelict Land Grant	Time:	1987-91
Reclamation of former colliery for residential development	Expenditure:	£1.24 million

Features

- Project assessment
- Development
- Amenity improvement
- Partnership
- Grant assistance

6.31 The site (38 acres) is situated to the west of Manchester, adjacent to the East Lancashire Road (A580) in an established residential area. The land was purchased by housebuilders from the National Coal Board and was formerly the site of the largest colliery in the United Kingdom. Although allocated in Local Plan policies for industrial development, planning permission for residential development was secured on Appeal.

6.32 The initial phase of development revealed substantial site problems including a deep overburden of colliery shale, mineshafts and shallow workings, lagoons and underground watercourses. The housebuilders applied and were granted Derelict Land Grant (private sector grant: 80% eligible costs).

6.33 The scheme when completed in 1992 will comprise 200 dwellings together with a public house and public open space. Derelict Land Grant costs will have totalled £1.24 million out of a total reclamation cost of £2.3 million and attracted private sector investment of £8.3 million. The development, which has attracted substantial private sector investment and made a major environmental contribution to the area, would not have been completed without grant assistance.

Features

Project assessment: the residential development potential was identified by the housebuilders who successfully achieved planning permission at Appeal. However, they substantially underestimated the extent and nature of the problems of dereliction of the site.

Development: the reclamation of the site was directly linked to the residential development scheme. Without private sector Derelict Land Grant it is unlikely that the developer would have progressed the project.

Amenity improvement: the scheme has removed the dereliction associated with formerly the largest colliery in the country. This has had a significant beneficial impact on surrounding residential areas. The provision of public open space has also been a benefit.

Partnership: the provision of assistance through private sector Derelict Land Grant has required an effective partnership between the developer and the private sector in undertaking this project.

Grant assistance: the financial assistance given to support the development has been essential for the scheme to proceed.

Casework study 14

St Peters Marina, Newcastle

Urban Development Corporation
Reclamation of riverside dock for
residential and marina scheme

Time: 1987-91
Expenditure: £11.6 million

Features

- Project assessment
- Amenity improvement
- Grant assistance
- Promotion
- Partnership
- Development
- Infrastructure

6.34 The site (12 acres) is situated on the Tyne riverside, east of the City Centre. A former industrial and boat building yard, it is approached through an unattractive industrial environment. It is relatively isolated from neighbouring residential areas which include Local Authority peripheral housing estates nearby. The site was selected by Tyne and Wear Development Corporation as a 'flagship' project for reclamation and residential development in partnership with a housebuilder.

6.35 Following selection of a development partner the Urban Development Corporation undertook works to stabilise the site, together with sheet piling and excavation for the marina, provision of tidal gates and estate roads. The development reflects the Urban Development Corporation's strategic policies of removing riverside dereliction, attracting investment and people to the area, and promoting an extended riverside walkway and environmental corridor on completion . The scheme will provide 277 dwellings for sale, shared equity and rent, together with shops, offices and a marina.

6.36 Over two hundred dwellings have been sold to date. The cost of reclamation and other works has been high, £11.6 million, but has attracted private investment of £15.4 million, which will increase as the developer has now purchased additional land to extend the scheme, without further grant assistance. Some of the reclamation costs can also be offset against savings achieved through use of spoil as fill for another UDC project nearby. The scheme has successfully attracted private sector investment and home owners to a location which was seen as very unpromising.

Features

Project assessment: the potential for the site was identified by the Urban Development Corporation as a 'flagship project' as part of the comprehensive development plan for the Urban Development Corporation area. The potential for the scheme was subsequently confirmed by the selection of a developer to progress the scheme.

Promotion: the Urban Development Corporation successfully promoted the site for marina and residential development to the private sector.

Development: the site acquisition, reclamation and river frontage works are pre-requisites for residential development. The focus of the residential scheme on the marina and the river/frontage has provided an internal environment which offsets the adverse impacts of an unattractive entrance and poor quality neighbouring uses.

Highways and infrastructure: a significant element of the works was the repair of the dockside and waterfront walls.

Partnership: the works to the site have been integrated with the scheme being undertaken by the developers.

Grant assistance: the funding of the environmental works to the site has provided a development cost subsidy to allow scheme viability.

Casework study 15

St Peters Riverside, Sunderland

Urban Development Corporation Reclamation of dockyard for residential development	Time: Expenditure: Total Approved:	1987-91 £6.7 million £27 million

Features

- Project assessment
- Highways and infrastructure
- Grant assistance
- Promotion
- Amenity improvement
- Development
- Partnership

6.37 The site (60 acres) occupies an extensive frontage on the north side of the mouth of the River Wear. It included derelict docks and sea defences in poor condition, together with contaminants left by former industrial processes. The potential for shipbuilding or ferry use was examined, but were not viable. The original proposal by the Urban Development Corporation was a 'flagship' project for residential development of the North Docks. This has been extended to incorporate adjoining sites at North Sands, earlier reclaimed by the Local Authority, and also Manor Quay.

6.38 The Urban Development Corporation has planned a residential-led comprehensive development of the site, together with a marina, a managed workspace scheme developed by English Estates, a higher education campus facility for Sunderland Polytechnic, and visitor and retail facilities. A private sector development partner has been selected for the initial phase which will include a mixture of housing for sale, rent and shared equity, as well as sheltered housing.

6.39 With the commencement of the initial phase this ambitious project is at an early stage. The cost of reclamation, land and acquisition and sea defence works to date has been some £6.7 million, with an estimated further £27 million required. This includes costs which would be incurred in any event for coastal and sea defences. On completion the scheme is estimated to include private sector investment of some £80 million. The scale of development will radically transform the area and extend the range of housing choice, particularly in the higher quality and cost sectors.

Features

Project assessment: the residential development potential for the site was identified in the Urban Development Corporation's assessment of the area where it designated the scheme a 'flagship' project. This was confirmed by securing developer interest before the reclamation works commissioned.

Promotion: the site was promoted to the private sector by the Urban Development Corporation and a residential developer was successfully identified.

Development: site acquisition, reclamation and works to the dock walls were pre-requisites to the scheme. The developers would not have committed themselves to these works.

Highways and infrastructure: provision of access and the restoration of the dockwalls were an important cost element of the works undertaken.

Amenity improvement: redevelopment of the dockside area will make an important contribution to the amenity of the area and assist in its overall regeneration.

Partnership: the development has required the partnership of the residential developer and the Urban Development Corporation to progress the scheme.

Review of site project case studies

6.40 The concluding element of this section reviews the overall findings of the site project case studies and seeks to draw out some of the key messages in terms of:

- **A. CHARACTERISTICS:** (i) the evidence of the broad influences of the site project approach,
  (ii) use,
  (iii) scale, and
  (iv) different urban policy programmes

- **B. FEATURES:** the role of the individual features identified.

A. Characteristics

i. Site project appraisal

6.41 The site project approach is based on tackling individual sites and addressing their particular development constraints. As such it works within the local area context and economy and such constraints need to be recognised, at least implicitly, if the development objectives are to be realised. A formal project appraisal at the outset provides a framework for these judgements.

6.42 Importantly, if the wider benefits of site projects are to be achieved, for example demonstration effects, or impacts achieved over the surrounding area where possible, there needs to be consideration as to the linkage with other projects and programmes for the area.

ii. Use

6.43 The projects selected have involved single uses, commercial or residential. The different uses have had an influence on the impact of EIPs in the attraction of development investment.

> **Retail:** Individual retail site projects tend to be freestanding, although may take place in the context of wider area programmes. Developments such as supermarkets or superstores are of a scale and character which are substantially independent of their environments. The higher development values associated with these uses also tend to remove such projects from the need for EIP support. Where grant assistance is required, City Grant or previously Urban Development Grant is often available. EIP's may be required from an area programme context to link the site into the surrounding area and secure wider benefits.

> **Commercial:** The principal benefits from site specific EIPs for commercial uses (office, industry, hotels) are:

> - environmental enhancement encouraging higher use values (Clayton-le-Moors, Lancashire)

> - the availability of sites and services to which occupiers could not readily have access (Qualcast Site, Wolverhampton; Bentley Site, Walsall)

> - assumption of site reclamation risk and grant assistance towards development costs (Westwood Power Station, Wigan; Newhallhey, Rawtenstall).

6.44 A feature of the commercial projects examined is the increasing importance attached by occupiers to their environment - although it remains less important than issues of communications and site availability. The importance of environment from the occupiers' perspective remains understated, but to the extent that its importance is likely to increase it will place additional emphasis on the amenity aspects of EIPs in the future for commercial projects, even in the less attractive inner areas.

Residential: the experience of the case studies suggests that the principal benefits from site specific EIPs for residential development are similar to those for commercial development:

- environmental enhancement (St Peters, Riverside)

- availability of site and services (Black Lake, West Bromwich)

- assumption of site reclamation risk (Chad Road, Bamford)

- grant assistance towards development costs (Mosseley Common, Wigan)

6.45 However, the relative emphasis placed on environmental enhancement and grant assistance is less. Residential schemes can create their own internal environment which permits development in relatively unattractive locations (Black Lake, West Bromwich) if local demand exists. It is also apparent that at least three of the schemes required no grant assistance to achieve development viability - only that the public sector assumed the initial risk of reclamation costs. In appropriate locations therefore residential development offers the benefits of relative tolerance to adverse environs, and relatively higher returns to set against grant costs.

iii. Scale

6.46 The projects ranged in scale from in excess of 90 acres to under one acre. The general influences associated with size were:

- larger scale developments could support more extensive off-site works, such as road access and services - in essence assuming the advantages of scale associated with area projects (Westwood Power Station, Wigan)

- the scale of site constraints tended to increase with the size of the site, as in the case of adverse ground conditions (Mosseley Common, Wigan) although there were often some economies of scale in treatment or arrangement of development

- on all sizes of site it was possible to achieve a high quality internal environment through careful design and layout (Black Lake, West Bromwich)

- the larger scale projects required commitment over an extended timescale by the public agencies, reflecting phased expenditure and land release (St Peters Riverside, Sunderland)

The scale of projects had no particular implications for the impact of EIPs so far as the effectiveness of the projects was concerned.

iv. Urban policy regimes

6.47 **Urban Programme:** a feature of the site projects is that with the exception of schemes which were developed by Local Authorities where Urban Programme featured, the majority of the EIPs were either funded through Derelict Land Grant or Urban Development Corporations. City Grant is also a significant source of support for site specific private sector development. With Urban Programme private sector developers lack of information and an appreciation of the potential scope for participating with Urban Programme projects. Urban Programme is available to the private sector under the Inner Urban Areas Aact for conversion, modification or improvement of property. Promotion of assistance, however, depends on Local Authority initiative and is usually targetted at building occupiers and incorporated in area based approaches rather than site specific projects.

6.48 **Derelict Land Grant:** this was the major funding source for the EIP site projects selected, and also reflects the general position that DLG is the principal funding regime for public sector site improvement outside Urban Development Corporation areas. It is also important, to a lesser degree, in private sector site improvement. DLG cannot provide general deficit funding, unlike City Grant, because it is applied solely to site costs and cannot provide market support for development. However it has the potential to absorb higher site abnormal costs for schemes where development values are modest. The relative attractions of the different regimes to the private sector depend on individual projects and the balance of site costs and values. The simplicity of the Derelict Land Grant scheme is seen as attractive by the private sector, as contrasted with the more complex City Grant regime.

6.49 There is some evidence that the larger scale site reclamations remain beyond the scope of private sector DLG - both in terms of the costs involved and the scale of risk. Where large scale DLG projects arose, the private sector either assumed the lead having underestimated the scale of the problem (Mosseley Common, Wigan) or preferred to route the reclamation through public sector DLG (Townley Brickworks, Burnley).

6.50 **Urban Development Corporations:** the two case studies reviewed are both major site reclamation and infrastructure provision (St Peters Marina and St Peter's Riverside). Both schemes were undertaken in partnership with the private sector to ensure development investment was linked to substantial EIP commitment, and that there was an integrated programme of reclamation and development.

6.51 The scale of costs for the Urban Development Corporation projects is substantially in excess of any of the other projects. Importantly at this scale the Urban Development Corporation has the expertise and direction which can work confidently with the private sector. This is a major consideration in attracting private sector investment for such projects.

B. Features

6.52 **Project assessment:** all the projects were the subject of an initial feasibility assessment. For Derelict Land Grant and Urban Development Corporation projects this is formally incorporated in the appraisal for funding support.

6.53 In the case of Urban Programme property market and development feasibility is less formally reviewed. This has proved inadequate in one case where an initial repair grant was not secured on a clear assessment of the future potential of the building (Gerard Gamble Building, Nottingham) and the Council ultimately had to acquire the property for comprehensive refurbishment.

6.54 **Promotion and consultation:** consultation with owners, occupiers and surrounding businesses has been less of a feature with site project schemes as, in most cases, the site or premises are vacant. However, projects have benefited from consultation with adjoining occupiers and owners where the scheme can act as a focus for the promotion of wider area improvements (South Sefton Business Centre, Bootle) or where there is the potential to involve neighbouring owners with extended improvement of facades or boundaries (Qualcast Site, Wolverhampton).

6.55 Promotion of the development opportunities created by EIP works has been most effective when undertaken with a full planning and development brief and supporting technical information to seek to ensure that elements of risk associated with the site or planning, which may have deterred investment, are removed (Chad Road, Bamford; Black Lake, Walsall).

6.56 **Development:** all the sites promoted for economic regeneration have been for development projects on site. In three cases public agencies have had to undertake the development direct because of prevailing market conditions (Gerard Gamble Building, Daisyfield Mill, South Sefton Business Centre).

6.57 Overall, the development schemes which have been completed have been successful and reflect well on the EIP approval and appraisal procedures. The relative success of public agencies compared with private development is difficult to judge on the limited number of case studies. The South Sefton Business Centre development at Bootle has proved very successful and there is provision in the project to now attract private sector investment for the second phase. The Business Centre development at Blackburn (Daisyfield Mill) is still establishing itself, but the level of occupancy is rising. The Gerard Gamble building rehabilitation has not been completed at this stage.

6.58 **Highways and infrastructure:** only the larger projects have required EIP support for significant highway and infrastructure works. The balance of the sites have been capable of redevelopment without substantial expenditure of this type.

6.59 The requirement for new highways and infrastructure principally arises from the division of larger sites previously in single use and ownership, where existing arrangements and layout cannot support multi-occupation (GEC Site, Clayton-le-Moors: Newhallhey, Rawtenstall).

6.60 **Property rehabilitation:** only public sector agencies were responsible for rehabilitation schemes amongst the case studies. If undertaken by the private sector, these projects would have been eligible for City Grant. The lack of involvement of private sector development in rehabilitation reflects the additional problems associated with redevelopment of existing structures.

6.61 Two of the rehabilitation projects have had property rehabilitation as a subsidiary objective to economic regeneration (Gerard Gamble building, Daisyfield Mill). Both buildings were identified as being of merit, with Daisyfield Mill also having 'listed' status. Re-use of these buildings was seen as making a contribution to the surrounding environment.

6.62 **Amenity improvement:** with the exception of one site (Chad Road, Bamford) which was heavily screened, all the projects have made a contribution to the visual amenity of their environs. In the case of building rehabilitation this has involved retaining existing structures. In the case of sites with extensive dereliction (Westwood Power Station, Wigan; Towneley Brickworks Burnley) which were a visual intrusion, these have been removed. Land which contained quarries or mine shafts has also been made safe (Bentley Site, Walsall; Chad Road, Bamford).

6.63 The wider benefits on environs of improved amenity are difficult to measure, and are likely to be reflected in longer term perceptions of their environs. In some cases, the enhanced environment has encouraged a higher quality and value of development (GEC.Site, Clayton-le-Moors). However, this may also have required EZ benefits to allow higher levels of rent and specification to be achieved.

6.64 **Policy linkage:** the integration of site specific EIP schemes with wider public policy objectives, for example small business accommodation or accommodation for the textile industry (Gerard Gamble Building) is mostly confined to the public agency led projects. The principal exceptions are where the Local Authority and Tourist Board joined forces to promote development (Bentley Site, Walsall) and when a strategic site assessment identified the requirement for prestige large scale single occupier sites which promoted the proposals for land reclamation for a major site (Westwood Power Station, Wigan). In addition the reclamation of an industrial site for small scale occupiers (Qualcast site, Wolverhampton) was linked to economic development policy supporting local firms. The integration of wider public policy objectives for some projects has assisted their promotion and in some cases justified additional funding assistance.x

6.65 **Grant assistance:** the reclamation of land and buildings has provided direct subsidy for development in all but some of the residential sites (Black Lake, West Bromwich). In the case of these residential schemes the relatively high values and speed of development has been reflected in higher site proceeds which exceeded the cost of reclamation. This emphasises the point that in some circumstances it is the scale and risk of reclamation rather than the deficit cost that is a constraint on development. There remains therefore a strong case for public sector led reclamation even where the site development value in these cases may be positive.

6.66 **Funding mixture:** some of the larger scale EIPs have successfully drawn funding from a range of sources. These include Ubran Programme and ERDF as well as the use of City Grant for development. This has helped broaden the funding base.

7 Impacts of environmental improvements

7.1   This section takes the framework of development factors and the potential for EIP impact assessment (Section 2), and compares the findings of the developer survey (Section 3) and case studies (Sections 5 and 6) to identify the practical impact of EIPs with economic objectives on urban regeneration. This is examined under two headings:

- EIPs and the Development Process: how environmental improvements affect perceptions of potential investors.

- EIPs Structure and Context: the application and links between area and project specific urban regeneration, environment and different urban locations.

7.2   Our overall assessment is that EIPs with economic objectives do have an impact on urban regeneration in attracting development investment. The impact is influenced principally by: external factors, in particular the strength of the local economy and development demand; and thenature of EIPs, most directly the removal of individual site and area physical constraints.

7.3   The impacts of visual or amenity improvements alone are more diffuse and have less influence on economic regeneration, at least in the short term. These issues are explored further below.

EIPs and the development proicess

7.4   We identified a framework of the key factors which are elements of the development process (Section 2) and also identified their importance for different types of developers (Section 3). The effect of EIPs can be assessed in terms of each of the development factors. We have divided the factors between those where EIPs have the potential for stronger and weaker impacts.

Stronger impacts

7.5   EIPs have the greatest potential impact on the following development factors

Site and premises availability

7.6   All developers identified the importance of site and premises availability and how EIPs can influence this through site assembly and acquisition, clearance and disposal. The evidence of the case studies is that projects which included or were directly related to site provision could demonstrate immediate impacts. This emphasises the need for EIPs to address to site and area physical constraints as a priority.

> **Chad Road, Swan Village:** in common with some of the other residential projects, the project was self-financing with site proceeds exceeding reclamation costs. In theory, no public sector support was required. However, the preparation and promotion of the site were essential to attract private sector investment.

> **Blackbrook Valley, Dudley:** whilst developers and occupiers are supportive of the enhanced amenity of the area, the lack of linkage to development has meant that the economic impact of the project has to an extent been dissipated.

Site access, transport and infrastructure

7.7   EIPs influence developers' perceptions through the provision of enhanced site access, transport and accessibility. This encompasses off-site works which may benefit an area overall, or individual project-specific applications. Typical of the range of successful EIP case studies are pedestrianisation or improvements of highways and car parking where these are a constraint. Access is fundamental to the intensity and nature of land use. It is also a very visible commitment to the long term viability of an area. Again, such EIPs emphasise the importance of application and linkage with actual area and site physical constraints.

> **New Ferry, Wirral:** the pedestrianisation of the core retail area has enhanced shoppers' accessibility and this has been complemented by provision of car parking as part of the scheme.

> **Stoney Lane, Rainhill:** improvements to the industrial estate road have been the justification for business investment on the estate.

Land and development costs

7.8   An important influence on investment through EIPs is the subsidy provided to land and development costs to promote development viability.

Moseley Common, Wigan: without the funding assistance through private sector DLG, the residential development would not have proceeded to completion.

North Shields and Fish Quay, Tyneside: funding support has been essential to the provision of new handling facilities for the local fishing industry as part of the EIP programme.

Planning and economic policies

7.9   The impact of EIPs in changing perceptions is influenced by their promotion and support through complementary planning and economic policies. Development Control policies can provide pro-active support and a framework which encourages complementary uses and improved scheme design. The application of economic policies can draw in additional funding and allow public sector led development to contribute to environmental and economic regeneration.

Lace Market, Nottingham: Development Control policies to retain accommodation for textile companies has complemented EIP programmes to improve buildings and encouraged occupiers to reinvest in their businesses.

South Sefton Business Centre, Bootle: economic development policies have supported the provision of small office accommodation and a business services centre, promoted the conversion of a derelict building, and encouraged businesses in the area to consider improvements to their properties.

Weaker impacts

Location and accommodation requirements

7.10 EIPs may remove physical constraints to development and allow locations to compete for investment in the short and medium term. EIPs cannot directly influence location and accommodation requirements. The overall levels of development demand and its characteristics are imposed by external economic forces which are not subject to environmental management. This needs to be recognised in any programme of EIPs.

7.11   The depressed levels of investment in urban areas are often, in part, a reflection of the relative weakness in the local economy and are therefore an external constraint on EIPs' impact. Even where case studies have demonstrated significant development successes levels of demand impose a constraint.

Lace Market Nottingham: rentals for premises for the indigenous textile industry remain below the level where private sector investment is attracted - even with grant support.

> **Closegate, Newcastle:** office development will not be initiated without a pre-letting.

> **Mathew Street, Liverpool:** specialist retail development has proved difficult to sustain in the Cavern Walks scheme.

7.12   Looking to the longer term, it is possible to identify in general terms the potential impact of EIPs on local economic structure and therefore indirectly on overall levels of demand. As investment is attracted to a location this is turn will assist in strengthening and developing the local economy. This is considered further below.

Environmental requirements

7.13   EIPs with visual amenity emphasis, as opposed to removal of physical constraints to development, tend to have a weaker impact. Developers were generally of the view that occupiers' amenity requirements were focused on their immediate environs, and that occupiers' tastes, preferences and locational needs were not susceptible to influence through EIPs. Changes in environment, in terms of visual amenity, were not sufficient alone to have an impact on investment without potential developers' locational and accommodation criteria being satisfied. As such EIPs tended to reinforce investment decisions, and needed to be concentrated and closely linked to development for greatest effect.

7.14   The general evidence of case studies tends to support this. For example, residential development has been achieved in adverse environments and where a relatively low emphasis has been placed on surroundings by creating an improved local environment within the scheme.

> **Black Lake, West Bromwich:** a development of mid-price housing where the environs are unattractive and the site is dominated by a power pylon.

> **Blakeley Hall Gardens, West Bromwich:** where the residential development is in close proximity to the M5 motorway viaduct.

7.15   In seeking to enhance environments EIPs can assist by improving schemes immediate environs by taking advantage of existing assets, such as buildings, landscape or waterfront features. Waterfront development is perhaps the best example of using an inherently attractive feature as a focus for a successful development environment.

> **St Peters Marina, Newcastle:** whilst the approach and uses close to the development are unattractive, the residential development which has a waterfront focus has been very successful with a further phase planned.

> **St Peters Riverside, Sunderland:** the residential development is located in an area which has not supported private sector residential development before.

Quality and characteristics of land and buildings

7.16 A range of EIP instruments are designed to enhance the characteristics and quality of land and buildings and their visual amenity, for example through facade improvements and cleaning, walkway improvements or lighting. These projects may be desirable for amenity or social objectives, but their economic justification in affecting investment perceptions appears weak unless EIPs are linked to development or removal of physical constraints.

7.17 Developers are most influenced by the factors which are of direct and immediate impact: location and accommodation requirements, site access and availability and development viability. Factors such as site and building amenity are seen as within the developers' control in scheme design, and the potential involvement of third party agencies through EIPs is viewed as an additional complication. The impacts of enhanced amenity are discounted as too subtle and long term. The relative concentration of private sector investment on new build and comprehensive site development in the case studies may in part reflect this.

> **Whitworth Street, Manchester:** this is the only case study where building improvements (cleaning and floodlighting) were linked to private sector development. Developers considered the influence of EIPs to be marginal and emphasised the importance of grant assistance with development costs.

7.18 Occupiers and building owners in contrast appear more receptive to the influence of EIPs for amenity, which may reflect their continuing and long term connection with the area. For example, the take-up of improvement grants, apart from a subsidy on repairs, suggests that occupiers are more susceptible to EIP influence.

> **Mathew Street, Liverpool:** repair grants have been successfully promoted through Town Scheme and Urban Programme initiatives.

> **New Ferry, Wirral:** the take-up of repair grants was sufficiently strong that further applications were outstanding after the project was completed.

Surrounding environment

7.19 The impact of EIPs through improvement of the surrounding environment reflected the same considerations identified for the quality and characteristics of land and buildings, but on a larger scale.

7.20 Developers' decisions reflect the underlying assessment that environment is essentially a reflection of, and not a substitute for, economic regeneration. However, within that context different types of developer were more susceptible to EIP influence in improving the surrounding environment.

Whitworth Street, Manchester (Niche Developers): specialists in freestanding inner area projects did not find EIP improvements to the surrounding environment influenced their investment decision.

St Peters Marina, Newcastle (Urban Renewal): developers looked to EIPs' improvement in the surrounding environment to provide off-site infrastructure, access and services whilst seeking to provide an attractive environment within their schemes.

Closegate, Newcastle (General Developers): EIPs' improvements in the surrounding area were seen as important in reinforcing investment decisions and perceptions of the prospects for the area. This was evidenced in the hotel development at Closegate.

7.21 Occupiers have demonstrated a greater susceptibility to EIP influence through enhanced surrounding environments. Again, this may reflect a longer term commitment to an area.

New Basford, Nottingham: there has been significant investment in new premises and improvements to existing buildings.

Ouseburn, Newcastle: occupiers' perceptions are that the area is improving following sustained small scale environmental works to the surrounding area.

Economic structure

7.22 Whilst EIPs cannot directly influence location and accommodation requirements, in removing site constraints and building on locations' environmental assets, there is the potential to attract development investment. Over an extended period this will impact on the local economic structure and assist sustainable regeneration, but this often requires long term and continuing commitment. In this context, EIPs and development investment are important for retaining existing economic activity as well as encouraging investment from outside the area.

Qualcast Site, Wolverhampton: a local firm which was considering relocation out of the area has been attracted to the site, retaining employment and encouraging investment in new premises.

Westwood Power Station, Wigan: the attraction of Girobank with up to 600 skilled jobs will make an important contribution to the local economy. The wider local economic impacts arising from this investment will be substantial.

The potential for underlying change in an area is, however, substantially discounted by developers. Investment decisions are largely based on current or short term market assessment. Developers' emphasis is relatively short term. Whilst larger scale and more extended development projects may have reference to the potential uplift of an area, investment appraisal will usually place a substantial discount on these.

Availability of public finance

7.23 The potential availability itself of public sector support through EIPs is of limited attraction to the private sector. This, for example, contrasts with regimes such as Enterprise Zones which attract specialist developers and investment projects structured to maximise investment returns.

7.24 The principal reasons for this position are that EIPs under the regimes examined are for the most part initiated and implemented by the public sector. DLG is available to the private sector, but at a maximum of 80% of eligible works, compared with 100% of eligible works for the public sector. Urban Programme grant assistance is available as grants or loans to the private sector, but promotion through Local Authorities is often limited and partial.

7.25 Only two of the EIP schemes were initiated by the private sector.

> **Moseley Common, Wigan:** the development was conceived without private sector DLG, but an underestimate of site problems led to a requirement for grant assistance.

> **Towneley Brickworks, Burnley:** the reclamation scheme was initiated by the private sector but undertaken through public sector DLG.

Risk and timing

7.26 EIPs can influence investment through changing perceptions of risk and timing. The developers surveyed did not identify this as an influence, beyond general comments that perceptions of an area improving helped reinforce investment decisions. The case studies, however, give evidence of projects where EIPs have removed risk and thereby attracted investment. In particular, land reclamation which has been self-financing demonstrates how perceptions can be altered.

> **Towneley Brickworks, Burnley:** following reclamation the site was sold back to the owners for residential development at a cost exceeding reclamation.

> **Bentley Site, Walsall:** reclamation costs exceeded site value, but the hotel developer would not have undertaken the scheme without the public sector assuming the risk of reclamation.

Profile

7.27 There is limited evidence that EIP programmes will reinforce development decisions where associations with a 'flagship' project can enhance the developer's profile. Recent examples of formal Local Authority-developer partnerships confirm this. In the case studies examined, the larger scale 'flagship' projects were promoted by Development Corporations. Here some developers indicated in general terms that association with such projects was an influence, but in only one case was this specifically cited as a reason for pursuing the project.

St Peters Riverside: the prestige of the EIP scheme reinforced residential development investment.

Capital and rental values

7.28   The evidence that EIPs can influence investment decisions through supporting enhanced capital and rental values is limited and not supported by the developer survey. In one case study there is some evidence of enhanced values being achieved because of the quality of the EIP scheme which capitalised on other factors - notably EZ support and excellent road communications. Overall, the impact on values in relatively weak property markets would be difficult to establish, but there is evidence of increased occupancy following EIP schemes.

GEC Site, Clayton-le-Moors: the quality of the reclamation scheme and landscaping, supported by EZ benefits and immediate motorway access has encouraged B1 business space development as well as industrial and distribution uses on the site.

Newhallhey, Rawtenstall: proposed improvements for road access, together with wider environmental improvements in the area are likely to support B1 business space use in preference to industrial development.

7.29   Drawing together the experience of the various development factors there are a series of common themes which show that EIPs are effective in attracting development investment, but that their impact is influenced by wider circumstances.

- External economic and market factors influence development demand and therefore the potential impact of EIPs.

- EIPs have greatest economic impact where they are applied to removing physical development constraints. That is, for example, removing contamination, improving access, providing services or infrastructure, or making land and sites available.

- EIPs have weaker economic impact when they are solely focused on visual amenity without any relationship to physical development. That is that EIPs are too diffuse and subtle to achieve practical economic impacts at least in the short term.

EIPs structure and context

7.30   Within the overall examination of EIPs and their impact on urban regeneration, there are considerations as to whether their effectiveness is influenced by their application. In particular whether there is evidence reflected in:

Structure: the use of area programmes or site specific programmes

Context: different locations and development uses and locations.

Structure

7.31   The potential arrangement of EIPs in area programmes or site specific projects reflects:

- the economic development potential and constraints affecting the industrial area or site; and

- the management of EIPs and urban regeneration policy

- Economic development potential and constraints.

7.32   The balance of advantage between area and project specific approaches will depend on an assessment of the following factors in individual circumstances.

Development demand: whether the particular focus of development and investment is broadly or narrowly defined. For example, if investment is to be drawn from a wide range of existing businesses in an area then a broader based EIP strategy is appropriate (Ouseburn, Newcastle). If demand is more narrowly constituted then a more restricted site specific approach is appropriate, as in the case of small unit workspace projects (Daisyfield Mill, Blackburn).

Physical and functional integrity: a location may be defined by its physical and functional linkages. A site may be substantially self-contained with limited physical or functional linkages with its environs. In such circumstances, wider application of EIPs off-site will have limited relevance in terms of attracting investment, or of promoting area wide improvement (St Peter's Marina, Newcastle). Where a location has strong physical or functional linkages then these may be reinforced by EIPs in a broader area based approach, as is often the case for retail use (Hyson Green, Nottingham). Considerations of integrity may involve a single use, as in the case of a residential area based approach (Whitworth Street, Manchester). Equally, the potential for integration of complementary uses may suggest a wider approach (Castlefields, Manchester).

Area and site constraints: the nature of the constraints on development will need to influence the appropriate application of EIPs. Where constraints are site specific, for example access and services (GEC Site, Clayton le Moors) then an approach at this level is appropriate. Where constraints extend over a wider area, for example the requirement for grant assistance to rehabilitate buildings (Mathew Street, Liverpool) an area approach is more effective.

Resources: the nature and extent of the resources available relative to the constraints and development potential. If resources are spread to the extent that constraints are not being effectively addressed then this undermines efficiency.

7.34 The appropriate area programme or site specific approach will also depend on considerations of management and timescale.

Co-ordination: area wide programmes and multi-project EIPs are more difficult to co-ordinate and manage effectively. In particular, there is a need for a continuity of effort and momentum for more extensive projects, which was demonstrated in successful projects (New Ferry, Wirral). This approach may necessitate additional personnel and resource requirements.

Promotion: effective promotion of EIPs is important. The demonstration effects of action, and the encouragement of participation are important features in regeneration. Many private sector parties have not had experience in working with the public sector regimes examined. Thus the explanation and promotion of grants or programmed improvements needs careful development.

Integration: the impact of EIPs can be increased if reinforced by complementary planning and economic policies. In promoting and encouraging regeneration, such policies may include encouraging private sector support through financial contribution or integration of development with EIPs (Nottingham and Beeston Canal, Nottingham).

Timescale: in many locations, urban regeneration will take an extended timescale to become self-sustaining. There are, however, clear advantages in a continuing and concentrated commitment through EIPs in a location. Where resources have been applied too thinly over an extended area and timescale, momentum and direction have not been achieved, and the impact dissipated to some degree.

7.34 In conclusion, the appropriate structure and context of EIPs is dependent on the individual project circumstances. This places an emphasis on a clear understanding of local development potential and constraints to ensure that the appropriate EIP structure and objectives are identified.

Context

7.35 The context for each of the projects represents a unique combination of demand and supply considerations which reflect location and land use. At the general level, however, it is possible to identify some broad considerations on land uses and their relationship to the impact of EIPs.

- **Retail**

  Retail activity is sensitive to the quality of the surrounding environment. Retail environments are important in seeking to attract and retain shoppers in competition with other centres. The potential actions to

enhance retail environments are also relatively well defined, for exa[...]
pedestrianisation, improved parking and access, and provision of a[...]
appropriate range and mix of retail facilities. The retail centre is also an
important focus for the surrounding area. Retailing is, in principle,
predisposed towards economic development through environmental
works, subject to local factors such as available expenditure and
communications.

- **Residential**

  The immediate environment is important to residents. The layout and
  arrangement of schemes can often achieve an attractive and secure
  internal environment, creating or focusing on the best features even
  though the surrounding environment is unattractive. Also, in urban areas,
  there is often housing demand from those already resident or with an
  association with the area wanting to remain and purchase their own
  home. Some of the case studies selected have demonstrated that even
  where the approach to a site or adjoining areas offer a very poor
  environment, successful projects have been developed.

- **Business space and industry**

  Successful schemes reflect a wide range of factors, in particular
  communications, accessibility, and relationship to services. The
  surrounding environment is an influence, but it would appear to be only
  one factor and not the most important. What is apparent is that if all the
  other development factors are favourable, an enhanced environment can
  encourage higher quality of development and reduce property vacancy.

- **Hotel and leisure**

  The hotel and leisure case studies suggest that such developments are
  essentially freestanding from their surrounding environment. In the
  case of hotel projects, road communications and, where central, links to
  the City Centre are important as business custom is the principal market.
  The larger leisure schemes are attractions in their own right, and are
  also freestanding. The aim of environmental works should be to
  incorporate and consolidate these projects within the urban fabric to
  support other uses nearby.

- **Public open space**

  Public open space provides an important link and context for urban
  development. Substantial area development programmes often have
  the improvement or the creation of public areas together with
  infrastructure and services as a key feature. The most successful areas
  of public open space created in the case studies were those which had a
  strong relationship with adjoining development.

8 Conclusions

8.1   This section sets out our conclusions to the study in terms of:

- the objectives of EIPs promoted for economic regeneration

- the extent to which EIPs affect the attitudes and perceptions of potential investors

- the capacity of EIPs to help regenerate inner city areas, and the scale and capacity of environmental projects required

- the policy implications.

8.2   Our conclusions are that EIPs promoted for economic regeneration make a practical contribution to urban renewal in attracting and supporting private investment. The impact of EIPs is, however, substantially influenced by economic and market circumstances, and the application of EIPs to individual area and site constraints.

Objectives of environmental improvement projects

8.3   EIPs' objectives cover a broad range including economic, social, amenity, conservation and others. There is no consistent formal definition of EIPs which extends across the Urban Programme, Derelict Land Grant, and Development Corporation regimes. However, there is a clear group of economic environmental projects whose objectives are the improvement of land and buildings and the attraction of private investment.

8.4   The case studies were selected as examples of successful projects. Their objectives can be divided as follows:

- intermediate objectives which are the immediate outputs in terms of physical measures such as land reclamation, highways, floorspace;

- final objectives which are the ultimate outputs in terms of urban regeneration which may be measured in economic terms of employment retained or created, investment and other local economic measures.

Intermediate objectives

8.5   In all cases the projects have achieved the immediate objectives and outputs. There was no evidence of any general problems in achieving these objectives. With some of the more complex products additional resources were required where more extensive works were needed once works had started which is to be expected and each of the project regimes has formal systems for accommodating this.

Final objectives

8.6   The relative success of the projects in attracting economic investment and wider regeneration objectives varied. All projects were progressing in this direction, but their success was influenced by the following factors:

- the prevailing local economic conditions and development market demand

- the physical constraints on development and investment for the individual area or site and whether these were addressed by EIPs

- the application and management of EIPs.

8.7   These considerations are reviewed further in terms of the capacity of EIPs to influence attitudes and perceptions of potential investors and the capacity of EIPs to regenerate urban areas.

EIPs Influence on attitudes and perceptions of potential investors

8.8   The extent to which EIPs influence attitudes and perceptions of investors rests on their impact on individual development factors, the relative importance of these factors according to individual circumstances, and the overall context of sustainable economic development.

8.9   EIP's impact on development investment are strongest when addressing the following development factors.

- **Site and premises availability:** the assembly, clearance and servicing of sites, together with resolution of planning and ownership issues and promotion of development opportunities are a key element which can be influenced through EIPs.

- **Site access, transport and infrastructure:** EIPs are able to secure the improvement of the site location and access through highway works, pedestrian and vehicle separation schemes, car parking, mains services, and infrastructure to stabilise sites such as repair of retaining or dock walls or major off-site works.

- **Land and development Costs:** EIPs can provide an important development cost subsidy to allow scheme viability through the financing of site, reclamation or servicing works.

- **Perceptions of risk:** some general developers' investment decisions are reinforced by the action of EIPs and the perception that an area is improving.

- **Planning and economic policies:** the support of complementary planning and economic policies with EIPs provides for a co-ordinated approach to urban regeneration. However, developers' perceptions of the relationship between EIPs and promotion of policies generally are weak.

8.10 EIP's impacts on development investment are much weaker when addressing the following factors:

- **Location and accommodation requirements:** EIPs cannot effectively influence location and accommodation demand, and the overall volume of investment, at least in the short term. Therefore EIPs' potential must have reference to local economic circumstances.

- **Environmental requirements:** EIPs in improving visual amenity can help promote a distinctive location, enhance area perceptions of urban renewal for general developers which may reinforce investment decisions. However, improvements to amenity alone are not sufficient in themselves to promote urban regeneration.

- **Economic structure:** EIPs potential influence on structural change extends over too long a period to influence developers' investment decisions at the outset of urban regeneration. In the longer term cumulative investment assisted by EIPs may effect change.

- **Availability of public finance:** the availability of public funding can attract developer interest, although funding physical improvements rather than offering direct financial incentives exercises only a limited attraction. This is further weakened by the relatively limited contact between public agencies and the private sector in the planning and implementation of EIPs.

- **Surrounding environment:** the impact of amenity improvements such as landscaping, external repairs, and frontage improvements through EIPs depends on the nature of the investor:

  niche developers: these inner area developers specialise in freestanding projects, and working within the existing urban fabric and are not predisposed to the influence of EIPs' improvement of the surrounding environment

  urban renewal developers: with an emphasis on comprehensive development these developers look to EIPs for any improvements to the surrounding area to be principally in the form of site access, transport and infrastructure to provide a framework for comprehensive development

general developers and occupiers: these investors find environmental amenity works help reinforce investment decisions, and provide the confidence that longer term area improvement is sustainable provided the underlying economic potential of the area is there.

8.11 In conclusion, EIPs influence on potential investors and development investment is most effective when:

- there is underlying property demand such that the local economy can support new development

- EIPs are applied as a direct support to development investment through the removal of physical constraints: in particular making sites available for development, providing access and infrastructure, and where required, subsidising development costs

- EIPs delivery of environmental amenity improvements can assist reinforcing investment decisions, depending on the nature of thedeveloper. Such improvements are not sufficient in themselves without the satisfactory resolution of underlying economic demand and removal of physical development constraints

- EIPs are reinforced by the promotion and support of complementary planning and economic development policies and the consultation with the private sector

Capacity of EIP's to regenerate inner areas

8.12 EIPs have the capacity to support the economic regeneration of inner urban areas. The evidence of this capacity is demonstrated in the successful case studies examined. The success and extent of the capabilities of EIPs to support urban regeneration requires the translation of EIPs potential strengths to influence attitudes and perceptions of potential investors, identified above, into practical action.

8.13 The evidence of the case studies is that the capacity of EIPs to regenerate inner areas to best advantage rests on two sets of factors. These are listed below and considered subsequently.

8.14 **Characteristics:** the selection of the appropriate EIP structure needs to be based on the following considerations:

- Area or policy led approach

- Use

- Policy regime.

8.15 **Project features:** the application of EIP's is most effective when the following specific features are addressed:

- Project assessment

- Property rehabilitation

- Highways and infrastructure

- Development

- Grant assistance

- Amenity improvement

- Promotion and consultation

- Funding mixture.

8.16 **Characteristics:** the selection of the appropriate EIP structure and application needs to have reference to the individual characteristics of the location, the prevailing uses and the strengths of the different policy regimes.

Area or project led approach

8.17 The selection of an area or project approach depends on the individual circumstances and the considerations. These include:

- nature and scale of development potential

- physical and functional integrity of the location

- constraints: which may be area wide or site specific

- resources: the scale of resources, the policy regimes available, the potential for grant mixing

- management: the arrangements for co-ordination, promotion and integration of policy and resources

There is no advantage inherent in either approach. The case studies demonstrate that either approach may be appropriate depending on the individual circumstances. Nor is there significance in the relative size of projects. Success depends on the application of EIP's commensurate with the scale of the constraints on development.

Use

8.18 Different uses have affected the capacity of EIPs to influence investment decisions, although the general assessments need to be tempered in the light of local economic and property market circumstances.

Retail: most retail schemes are area based because of the extensive established retail stock, and the shared constraints on investment. Site specific retail projects often generate sufficient return so as not to require EIP support. The key features associated with retail based EIPs are:

- retailing responds well to EIP area management

- as a dynamic sector there is often scope for relatively swift response to appropriate EIP action

- food retailing remains relatively resilient in adverse economic circumstances

- the retail stock is often dominated by owner occupiers or small investors who are amenable to EIP influence. Building repair grants are often used to lever investment

- pedestrianisation, footpaths, traffic management and parking schemes can often secure significant improvements to centres.

Commercial: there is evidence that commercial development is becoming more sensitive to its environment and the influence of EIPs on investment:

- the response to EIPs tends to be relatively slow because of the range of different interests involved and the prevailing lower development returns compared with retailing.

- EIPs have worked satisfactorily on both area and project bases

- highway improvements and off street parking and servicing are frequently linked as part of the programmes

- environmental enhancement has encouraged take up of accommodation, although evidence of securing higher quality use values is limited.

- servicing new development can be expensive relative to development values.

- some cases have required site clearance simply on the basis of risk rather than development subsidy

8.19 **Hotel and leisure:** these projects are essentially freestanding and either constitute a site specific project or are incorporated as a project within a wider area based approach.

- The projects require an operator involvement and cannot be pursued speculatively.

- EIP's can assist in providing physical linkages between such projects and the spin-off benefits of extending local services is helpful to the wider local economy.

8.20 **Residential:** almost all the residential developments assisted by economic EIPs are freestanding schemes. They can usually be grafted onto established residential areas, or if of sufficient size be established as freestanding development:

- residential development appears relatively insensitive to its environs

- site proceeds on reclamation are swiftly realisable and can often exceed reclamation

- development can be implemented over a short timescale.

8.21 The appropriate development use will depend on the individual site, but overall the fastest impacts are shown in retail area based EIPs and residential project based EIPs.

Policy Regime

Urban Programme

8.22 The regimes' strengths have been area-based and public sector project-based schemes.

Area based schemes: the most successful schemes have involved rigorous initial area assessment followed by a clear development plan. Extensive consultation and promotion has encouraged private sector participation. The impact of projects has been weakened without clear planning and programming.

Project based schemes: the site schemes have been successful and executed on the basis of market and development assessments. In most cases such schemes have also formed an element of wider area initiatives - thereby providing an important development focus and initial momentum.

8.23 With the movement towards larger scale projects this places increasing emphasis on consultation and promotion with the private sector. In this connection there is a weakness in the general understanding by the private sector of the operation and capabilities of Urban Programme, outside specific initiatives.

Derelict Land Grant

8.24 The focus of DLG EIPs is on project specific land reclamation by the public sector, for subsequent private sector development. In more limited cases, private sector DLG has been used, but the lower levels of grant eligibility are less attractive. The temporary transfer of site ownership to the public sector for higher levels of funding has allowed the more complex privately owned schemes to be brought forward.

8.25 The area based projects examined here have not had a strong linkage with development or been promoted to the private sector, being essentially amenity schemes. The impact of these schemes might be enhanced if they were used to promote wider improvements with participating owners and occupiers in the area, linked, if appropriate, with grant support.

Urban development corporation

8.26 The integration of EIPs with planning and economic development policies and strong promotion and profile has assisted the success of projects. The emphasis on site provision, access, and infrastructure works - usually on a substantial scale has worked well in meeting the needs of private sector investment - in particular urban renewal developers.

8.27 Where projects have had an amenity rather than development focus the impacts on private sector investment have not appeared so strong, at least in the short term.

Features

8.28 The particular features which have contributed to the most successful projects reflect the strengths and ability of EIPs to influence certain factors in the development process, and in particular the removal of physical constraints to development.

Area or project assessment

8.29 The rigorous assessment of economic and development potential at the outset of a project has been critical in establishing clear objectives, constraints, programme and timescale. Without this, projects, particularly without a specific development focus, have had a tendency to lack clear direction.

Development

8.30 Projects whose immediate focus has been development in terms of site provision or promotion of development have provided the immediate opportunity for private sector investment and the benefits of a demonstrable commitment to a location.

Highways and infrastructure

8.31 Improvements in land accessibility and the management of traffic and pedestrian movement have had a major impact in attracting development investment and improving locations' economic prospects.

Property rehabilitation

8.32 Promotion of grants for repair and improvement have been effective where provided to building occupiers, or owners of buildings in occupation. Their impact has been most effective where concentrated on key frontages and on the basis of an assessment of an area or project economic sustainability.

Grant assistance

8.33 Grant subsidy to development, particularly on site works such as reclamation, estate road and services, has been essential elements in securing development viability.

Policy linkage

8.34 Projects have benefited from the support of complementary development control and economic development policies, linking with other agencies to promote local economic development, extending the grant funding base, and safeguarding buildings and their urban context.

Promotion and consultation

8.35 The strongest projects have involved continuing consultation and promotion when seeking to engage the private sector, providing an exchange of information on proposals, and grant assistance.

Amenity improvements

8.36 Amenity improvements have had their greatest impact when linked with other projects, in particular development or site access improvements. They have been most influential when targeted at the attraction of investment from general developers or occupiers. Niche and urban renewal developers' investment decisions are not significantly influenced by such projects.

Partnership

8.37 Recently there have been formal partnerships established as joint ventures between the public and private sectors. This provides for enhanced co-operation and direction of investment into key projects and areas.

Programming and Timescale

3.38 These have been essential for area-based EIPs. Where these have been lacking then the more complex projects have tended to lose momentum and direction.

Policy implications

Funding mixture

8.39 Associated with policy linkage have been the benefits of funding mixture which extends the potential resource base for grant assistance.

8.40 EIPs impact on urban regeneration and the capacity to influence potential investors has policy implications. The effective application of EIPs needs to reflect the following considerations.

Area and project assessment

8.41 There is a requirement for an initial assessment of economic development potential before EIPs are designed and implemented. Such an assessment should define:

- economic and development potential

- constraints

- EIP selection area or site specific.

8.42 It is in this context that the choice between area programme or site specific EIPs needs to address the potential and constraints specific to an individual location. In identifying the appropriate approach explicit reference will be required in terms of:

- Physical and Functional Integrity: the linkages which define the potential and constraints of an area or site.

- Resources: the nature and extent of the EIP resources which can be made available to address potential and constraints, and the scale of activity implied.

Uses

8.43 The area or project assessment of potential and constraints will need to reflect the characteristics and uses in the area. The experience of the case studies implies that certain uses will respond more readily to different EIP approaches and this should inform their application.

Area led approach: Retailing
Commercial (Offices)

Site specific approach: Residential
                             Commercial (Industry)
                             Leisure (Hotels and Commercial Leisure)

Consultation and promotion

8.44 Effective consultation with and promotion to potential investors is required at three levels:

- initial consultation and discussion with land owners and occupiers and potential investors

- information and promotion during EIP implementation

- promotion of development opportunities to potential developers.

8.45 The use of initial consultations not only seeks to involve interests in defining constraints and opportunities. It also provides the potential to promote and test EIP options and investment opportunities.

8.46 Information and promotion is difficult to sustain over an extended period of implementation. Consideration needs to be given as to whether implementation timescales can be foreshortened to maintain momentum and impact.

8.47 Effective promotion of development opportunities means marketing projects to investors and providing full information on site or property conditions, planning, ownership, and potential grant assistance to support informed investment decisions.

Development

8.48 Priority needs to be given to identifying sites with investment potential - refurbishment or new build. These may include properties in occupation which would benefit from improvement, such as repairs or car parking. These would also include new development. The aim is to design and implement EIPs addressed to the needs of the specific investor or occupier rather than less focused generic improvements to an area. The scale and form of development needs to complement and support surrounding uses.

Highways and infrastructure

8.49 The potential and requirements for improvement of a location's accessibility and services to support economic development are a priority in seeking to attract private sector investment. Consideration of EIPs in this context needs to be a key element in framing improvements.

Property rehabilitation

8.50 EIP assistance with property rehabilitation needs to be linked to the requirements of owners and occupiers. If public sector investment is to be undertaken for sustainable regeneration it has to be concentrated on properties which have a potential use at least in the foreseeable future and which can be supported by the local economy and property market demand.

Amenity improvements

8.51 These need to be linked to the major physical elements of any EIP programme, that is development (site assembly, clearance, construction or refurbishment) and highways and infrastructure (site access, pedestrianisation, car parking, waterfront improvement). Their implementation needs to follow the completion of these elements so that they can be effectively integrated with major physical improvements where required, and effectively targeted at general developers and investors.

Policy linkages

8.52 EIPs must have reference to complementary programmes and policies to seek to focus initiatives on the locations identified as having potential for urban regeneration, and to achieve effective co-ordination of effort.

Partnership

8.53 Where there is scope for area based EIPs or larger site specific projects the public sector can benefit from formal partnership with the private sector to channel investment into specific locations, and to co-ordinate a partnership response to specific development opportunities.

Grant assistance

8.54 EIPs' provision of grant assistance helps offset development costs to secure the development viability of site specific projects, in particular site reclamation and servicing. To ensure that this is effectively directed places emphasis on the importance of the initial area or project assessment to clearly identify economic and physical development potential at the outset.

Programming and timescale

8.55 EIPs need to be effectively programmed with a timescale for implementation as part of the initial area or project assessment to ensure that objectives are met and direction maintained.

Funding mixture

8.56 Associated with policy linkages needs to be clear consideration of the range of funding sources and their application. This may include the involvement of other agencies, or the promotion of other grant regimes with particular development opportunities, such as City Grant.

Implications for inner city programmes and policies

8.57 EIP's with economic objectives have been demonstrated to be effective in supporting urban regeneration. Drawing together the conclusions of this study the implications for the effective application of economic EIPs for urban regeneration are set out opposite.

Area assessment

8.58 Before initiating EIPs there needs to be a definition of a location's economic, property market and development potential based on

- physical and functional linkages of the area and uses

- location and accommodation demand

- property availability, conditions and use

- highways, services and access.

8.59 Set against this, a definition of constraints can be made including

- highways, access and services

- property availability

- building repair and condition

- physical and environmental constraints.

- planning policies

8.60 These provide the basis for identifying the objectives of EIPs in addressing the location, and the appropriate scope as an area programme or site specific project.

8.61 Targeting EIP investment should take place within the area assessment context and address the potential sources of private sector investment.

- **Niche developers:** the development opportunities promoted to these developers will be essentially freestanding. These opportunities should be priorities for early promotion and may not require EIP support except in limited cases of site assembly and clearance.

- **Urban renewal developers:** the requirement is for highways and infrastructure EIP support for comprehensive development schemes. In these circumstances, EIPs should be targeted at those projects to promote investment, together with site assembly and clearance if required.

- **General developers:** after the highway and infrastructure improvements are in place, amenity improvements can be programmed to promote development opportunities to general developers.

There are also considerations in relation to the individual regimes.

8.62 **Urban Programme:** there is the need to make explicit the linkage between the objectives and the specification of EIPs and a location's potential and constraints. Economic EIPs have been weakest where there has not been a definition of area potential and context and the relationship of EIPs to this. This should take the form of an area assessment which identifies specific economic objectives and outputs.

8.63 **Development Land Grant:** the regime provides for assessment of development value of completion of reclamation for economic (land end use) projects. For some projects this has been linked to an assessment of location and accommodation demand and the potential requirement for associated EIPs, if required. This could be usefully adopted as a formal requirement.

8.64 **Urban Development Corporations:** the Urban Development Corporation plans provide for linkage between an area assessment and economic EIPs. In some cases the linkage between economic amenity projects and development could be made more explicit and this would assist in focusing economic project objectives.

Programming and timetable

8.65 There is a requirement for programming and timetabling EIPs on the basis of the area assessment and defined objectives. This already takes place for single EIPs, but where a programme is intended, in some cases these have been implemented incrementally or on the basis of an evolutionary programme which undermines coherent planning, co-ordination and effective promotion of the area's improvement.

8.66 **Urban Programme:** restrictions on project commitments extending beyond the financial year have encouraged short term and disjointed programming for some area projects. Relaxation on extended programme commitments where appropriate would assist

8.67 **Derelict Land Grant:** the concentration on site specific EIPs and the use of rolling programmes has assured programming and timetabling are maintained.

8.68 **Urban Development Corporations:** programming and planning over the lifetime of an Urban Development Corporation provides a formal framework.

Area and project use

8.69 The specification of EIPs depends on an individual location's economic and development potential and constraints. However, the predisposition of uses to environmental improvements suggests that the emphasis and economic EIPs should be applied in these areas:

> **Retail:** area programme improvements including pedestrianisation, improved parking, amenity improvements and complementary development, such as food stores.

> **Commercial:** area programme improvements, in particular highways and services; site specific projects, in particular site assembly and clearance, and access.
> **Residential:** site specific projects, in particular site assembly, clearance and servicing.

> **Leisure and hotel:** site specific projects, in particular site assembly clearance and servicing.

Consultation and promotion

8.70 Effective consultation and promotion is required throughout EIP programmes. In the case of area programmes it is essential that this is undertaken in conjunction with the area assessment as an input to identify potential and constraints, working with land owners and occupiers. There is also the opportunity to involve developers and agents in testing development opportunities, in principle. This may be undertaken informally, or in the case of larger area based projects a panel might be formed as a vehicle for encouraging participation and investment.

8.71 Promotion can be effectively undertaken on two levels - area and site specific. Newsletters and other material can inform and promote area based initiatives and to assist consultation and involvement. On a site specific basis development briefs providing full information on development potential, planning policies, ownership, site conditions, availability and grant assistance assist the promotion of opportunities.

Highways infrastructure and services

8.72 Adequate highways and supporting infrastructure are essential to promoting investment in inner areas and supporting development. An integral part of the area assessment is the identification of potential for improvements and removal of constraints, either through EIPs, or co-ordinated with other programmes.

113

8.73 Urban Programme and Derelict Land Grant: Local Authorities need to ensure that there is effective co-ordination between EIP and highway and services programmes to ensure priority and effective integration is achieved.

8.74 Urban Development Corporation: the designation of a Urban Development Corporation as highway authority provides for the effective integration of highways, services and environmental works. Where the Local Authority retains responsibility, arrangements are required to ensure co-ordination.

EIPs and site availability

8.75 For the effective application of EIPs to attract development investment it is essential that there is site availability. This requires, where necessary, the acquisition of sites by the public agencies if development is to be attracted to marginal locations.

8.76 Urban Programme: where EIPs are linked to development of key sites it is essential that site availability can be provided, working with land owners to promote development. Unless this can be assured then regeneration cannot take place.

8.77 Derelict Land Grant: site acquisition and clearance is undertaken through negotiation with land owners. The use of DLG powers to promote site availability could be broadened by the promotion of wider use of agreements to purchase and sell back land to owners after reclamation through public sector DLG, linked to development agreements.

8.78 Urban Development Corporations: vesting ownership and compulsory acquisition and powers already provide Urban Development Corporations with effective powers to ensure site availability.

Amenity improvements

8.79 Following highways and infrastructure, and site availability and clearance, amenity improvements are effective in attracting investment by general developers and occupiers. Amenity improvements for economic regeneration need to be linked specifically to development or investment projects to attract investment. Thus building repairs or facade improvements must be linked to private sector investment, and landscaping or planting relate directly to development projects. General area improvements may be desirable for other objectives, but are not sufficiently targeted to assist investment in urban regeneration.

Planning and economic framework

8.80 EIPs need to be supported and integrated with wider planning and economic policies where possible. These need to combine promoting area and site opportunities, with the objective of enhancing the amenity of the area.

Fund mixing

8.81 EIPs specification should identify the opportunities for attracting complementary funding from other sources, and how this is to be integrated. The aim is to diversify programme funding where possible and to provide for additional works where appropriate. Where they are available to the private sector, these should be promoted as part of a development/investment package.

8.82 In conclusion, the impact of EIPs with economic objectives is dependent on a clear assessment of economic and development potential and the constraints to be addressed, and the application of improvements to promote sustainable regeneration, with emphasis on highways and infrastructure, site availability and clearance, and amenity improvements in support of development.

Appendix I Developer Survey

The following development companies kindly participated in the study interview programme.

AJ Mucklow
Grosvenor Laing Urban Renewal
Inner City Enterprises
Leech Homes
Peel Holdings
Pilkington Properties
St Modwen
Shearwater
Slough Estates
Tay Homes

Printed in the United Kingdom for HMSO
Dd 0298602 C9 6/95